THIRTY YEARS ON TWO WHEELS

A Biking Odyssey

12/12/18
To Richie, one of the truly great
men of Boston –
with much admiration,
Tim

Julie Hatfield & Timothy Leland

Wasque Point Publishing
Portland, ME

To Christian, Juliana, Sasha, Jason and London

And to our friends Sumner and Helen Winebaum,
with whom we shared many lovely backroads

"I thought of that while riding my bicycle."

-Albert Einstein on the Theory of Relativity

Table of Contents

Preface

In the old days (that's when we were young), bicycling was for kids. Once you turned twelve or thirteen, you either gave your bike to a younger sibling or your parents gave the bike to a charity. Adults did not bicycle. Children did. Once you were a teenager you were finished with kid stuff.

So it was with us.

We never thought about bicycles, or biking, for the next 35 years.

Fast forward to 1983, when we met a friend who had just returned from an unusual European honeymoon. She and her new husband had signed up with a company that guided adults through the French wine country on bicycles, staying in historic chateaus, stopping for frequent wine tastings, enjoying fabulous French meals in local restaurants, smelling the flower-scented air as they rode through the countryside.

Her eyes sparkled as she talked about this new way of seeing France, and we were captivated, listening to her. Every morning after breakfast she and her husband started off with the other twelve people in the group, and every morning half an hour later the other twelve people had gone their separate ways at their own separate speeds. She and her husband were left to ride alone in perfect peace, just what they wanted on their honeymoon. They always managed to get to their next chateau by dinnertime after a day of private exploration and adventure.

Shortly after hearing her story we contacted the touring company she mentioned – Butterfield & Robinson, from Toronto – and the following May, we embarked on a B&R bike trip to Bordeaux.

We were both in our 40's and neither one of us had been on a bike for decades.

Smugly, we didn't think we needed to practice before our 10-day trip. Yes, it was going to be up and down the hills of Bordeaux, biking from 25 to 50 miles per day. But biking was kid play, right? It wasn't really a sport.

We didn't even wear helmets then, and we certainly didn't have biking shoes or shorts.

We were just going out to play, the way we used to ride our bikes on the street in front of our house.

We were in for a surprise. We learned on that first trip that biking is indeed a sport, and that you had better do some training if you're going to take a trip that involves eight hours on two wheels every day for a week.

We learned another thing on that first trip: biking is a sublime way to see a country - the best way of all, in our opinion.

This book, based on articles we wrote for the travel section of the Boston Globe, attempts to tell you why.

BORDEAUX, FRANCE

The husband's first day on the road.

Bordeaux

The Husband's Story

July, 1984

Our French bicycle tour began, for me, approximately 3,400 miles away in a Cambridge bike shop, where I went two days before we left Boston to buy a pair of bicycle shorts. Something simple. Something with pockets. Something soft in the rear end. Unfortunately, they didn't have what I was looking for. The only thing available was a pair of racing shorts, a skin-tight number made out of shiny blue nylon that tried to hide a spreading middle-aged paunch, and failed.

"You'll love the feel of them," the salesman confided. "You wear them without anything underneath." I took his word for it.

That evening I modeled them at home.

"Dad," my eight-8-year-old daughter said after an embarrassed silence. "You look a little weird."

My 15-year-old son was more emphatic. His assessment sounded like the final word:

"I hate to tell you, Dad, but you look like a total and utter fool."

The splendid old castle glimmered luminously in the afternoon sun as we drove up the long curving driveway.

Julie and I had come to Bordeaux from Paris on a high-speed express train. The urban sprawl of the capital had gradually given way to the lush colors of the French countryside as we sped past the red shingled roofs of little farms, grazing cows, the groves of stately poplars, ancient-looking churches with delicate spires, patchworks of emerald green fields and occasional squares of yellow mustard flowers so bright they dazzled the eye.

Now we were arriving by bus at the chateau in Camiac, where we would spend the first night of our tour and pick up our 10-speed bicycles.

Except for the occasional trip to the paper store on my son's bike, I hadn't been on one of these two-wheel contraptions for decades. The last one I owned had balloon tires.

"By the end of this trip," said Sally Meech, 27, one of our two guides, "you're going to think of your bike as a dear friend and companion."

The bike with my nametag on it was fire-engine red, with no-nonsense conventional handlebars. It looked like a dear friend and companion already, but I wondered if we'd still be on speaking terms at the end.

When I got up on top of it for the first time, its feather-light frame and finger-thin tires (whatever happened to tires with a little meat on them?) tottered precariously as we all took a practice spin on nearby roads. Somehow I made it around the track and got back to the chateau in one piece. My confidence soared. This French adventure would be easy,

But two hours later, at our group's fancy introductory dinner, I wasn't quite so sure. Riding a bike in France is one thing. Ordering wine, it turns out, is another.

By count, there were 184 wines to choose from at the Michelin two-star restaurant we dined at that evening. Intimidating, perhaps, for the average person, but no big deal for someone who has taken a course at the Boston Center for Adult Education, as I recently had, on "Buying Good Wines for Under Fifteen Dollars."

Julie looked impressed when I ordered a 1968 Chateau Latour-Pauillac for 1,600 francs. That's $16.00 I thought to myself, marveling at how inexpensive vintage wine was in Franc.

I decided to up the ante. Why not splurge a little? It's our first night here.

"Let's live it up," I said to the table - and changed the order to a 1974 Margaux for 1,700 francs.

According to my calculations, that was still only a couple of dollars over the magic fifteen-dollar cutoff I had set for our budget.

The waiter emerged a few minutes later holding my $17 bottle of wine like a delicate flower, cradling it in gentle hands. I was surprised to see how very dusty the bottle was. Even more so watching him proceed to decant it, carefully holding a candle beneath the glass, watching for the sediment inside.

It was at this point during the dinner that I fell very quiet, according to Julie. Sitting across the table from me, she noticed that I was no longer making casual conversation with the other tour members, and wondered why. There was a good reason. I was too busy doing grammar school arithmetic. Slowly, it had begun to dawn on me that I had misplaced a decimal point.

This wasn't a $17 bottle of wine I had just purchased for my new friends at the table. Mon Dieu, it was a $170 bottle of wine!

I woke up this morning feeling a bit under the weather. My two-star meal last night (the puree of native oysters and caviar, the lamproise in prune sauce,

Downhill is more fun than uphill.

the watercress salad, the endless assortment of cheeses, the endless choice of dessert pastries, the endless succession of after-dinner sweets and the endless quantity of wine, Margaux and otherwise) left me with a two-star hangover.

But the back roads of Bordeaux beckoned. We had our map. We had our directions. We knew our destination: St. Emilion, 20 miles to the east.

Julie and I set off.

How can one describe the pure delight of pedaling through the French countryside on a beautiful spring morning after 247 working days in a newspaper office?

We are alone with our thoughts, bicycling slowly down the narrow lanes, past quaint little farmhouses, past stone churches, past groups of women working in the fields, past lone farmers in black rubber boots who stare quizzically as we go by, through mile after mile of green vineyards. There is no traffic here. There are scarcely any cars, in fact. More than anything else one is struck by the tranquility of the scene, the wet earth steaming in the hot sun as we glide silently through the land.

In the lovely old town of St. Emilion, where we arrived shortly after noon, we visit the ancient church hollowed out from the side of a cliff. We have a light lunch of jam crepes in a small café, then sit on a stone wall in the spring sunshine for a few minutes, resting. Mid-afternoon we head back to our castle along a different route.

The group stops at an ancient chateau for a wine tasting along the way, and I linger for an additional splash of the heavy red burgundy. (One doesn't become a wine connoisseur without great effort.) By the time I get back on my bike, the rest of the group, including my wife, has left without me. They are somewhere up ahead.

I'm on my own. No problem.

After a morning of practice, I am an accomplished bicyclist. All I have to do is put my beautifully conditioned body into high gear and catch up to them.

My powerful leg muscles take over, each thrust of the thighs propelling the bike forward. The bike responds to the rhythmic synchronization of bone and muscle. There is perfect harmony of man and machine as I gain effortlessly on my distant companions.

I am Greg Lemond, the American bicycling champion.

I am Alexi Grewal, the Olympic Gold medalist.

I am Bernard Hinault, five-time Tour de France winner!

Sprawwwngg!!

My body lurches forward, all resistance to foot pressure gone. There is a terrible screeching sound, like ripping metal... I am a bald, middle-age man who doesn't know the first thing about bicycles, standing on a deserted road somewhere in the middle of France with a bicycle chain that has jumped its rear spindle and hangs beneath the bike like a disemboweled intestine.

Twenty minutes and a painfully pinched finger later, I finally figure out how to put the chain back on the sprocket. I get under way again, pedaling slower. My wife and the rest of the group are sitting around a grassy veranda, drinking white wine by the time I finally make it back to the castle for dinner.

It's the start of a new day and spirits are high, the indignities of last evening's mechanical failure mellowed by a luxurious sleep in our king-sized bed.

The white plastic bottle we each carry on our bikes is filled with mineral water, my handlebar bag carefully packed with extra film and a bar of Swiss chocolate.

The grass around the chateau is sparkling with dew as we prepare to set off for Bergerac, 70 kilometers away.

I wheel out my sleek red machine, check the tires for pressure. Perfect.

It's time to go. I glide a few feet down the castle driveway on one leg, then swing the other leg up over the bar and settle on the seat. Gary Cooper mounting his steed at high noon.

Ach! A sharp pain stabs through my body. Someone is jabbing at my crotch with a hot iron. A mysterious intruder has left shards of glass on my bike seat during the night. I've been mortally injured.

It turns out to be something different, however. My "avoirdupois" (as we say in polite French circles) is merely suffering from Bicyclers' Bruise. In other, less refined circles, it's known simply as a sore ass - and virtually everyone else in our group, I learn, has the same thing.

"The third day is always the worst," says Peter Chittick, our male tour guide. "By the last day you won't even feel it." That may be so, but in the meantime remedial action is required. My sweatshirt becomes a partial solution, folded up in a nice soft ball to aid the afflicted and comfort the wounded. I set off again, perched gingerly on the bike seat.

Bicycling through Bordeaux in the spring is like drifting slow-motion down an endless kaleidoscope of constantly changing colors.

As the sun climbs to midday, we pass through zones of fragrance that hang over the land in layers: The heavy smell of newly cut grass; the lighter, musky smell of stacked hay; the redolent sweet fragrance of spread manure; the powerful smell of wet earth; and, occasionally, a sharper, acrid small, the smell of burning grapevines.

We follow the meandering Dordogne River, stopping for a light lunch of wine and cheese at a small cafe, then head for Tremolat. Now come some hills. The pedaling gets harder. They seem to get longer and steeper, and I begin to perspire. Profusely. By 4 o'clock in the afternoon, I've become aware of another smell, a body fragrance that comes from the sweat that has soaked through my shirt and socks.

Julie, bless her Midwestern stamina, looks fresh as a rose - but this middle-age male flower is definitely beginning to wilt.

At 5 o'clock, thank goodness, a spring shower suddenly opens up and we have to take shelter under a tree.

I'm not about to tell Julie how delighted I am to see the B & R van that appears moments later, in the rain, to take us to our Bergerac hotel. In my exhausted state, a Red Cross ambulance couldn't have been more welcome.

"I'm glad you came for us," I tell Sally, as I heave my bike inside and jump in the front seat. "I was afraid Julie wouldn't make it."

A soft misty rain is falling over Bergerac this morning as we set off for Chateau Monbazillac four miles away. The schedule calls for another wine tasting session. What else is there to do at 10 a.m. in Bordeaux, after all?

In the inner sanctums of chateaus with names familiar from labels seen in the larger Boston liquor stores, we learn how wine is produced. It's a long and sophisticated process, as explained to us by the experts - or "vignerons" - who do it for a living.

The cool musty cellars all have the same slightly acrid smell, a combination of fermenting wine and the huge oaken casks that the wine is aged in. Even to an oenophile beginner like myself, there is something almost mystical about a glass of wine taken directly from one of these barrels, which lie in long rows like fat beached whales.

The rain has turned into a light drizzle by the time we have finished our tour of the chateau, a massive 16th-century castle with enormous moss-covered turrets, brooding darkly on the top of a hill.

Julie and I set off for Tremolat via the village of Faux. An hour later, pedaling silently through lush green countryside with no towns in sight, we pass a nondescript sign beside the road: "Bouniaques."

I stop and check the map attached to the top of my handlebar bike bag.

Bouniaques? I stare at the map, tracing our route with my finger. Where is

French pastries are a biker's fuel.

Bouniaques? Our notes don't say anything about Bouniaques.

Finally I see the town on the folded paper. At the bottom left margin. It's in the wrong direction.

"How could we be near Bouniaques?"

The answer is simple. We've taken the wrong turn and are far off course. That's easy to do on a B&R bicycle tour. The roads traveled are small and the route signs obscure. The turns on the map are easy to miss. And when it happens there's nothing to do except grin and bear it. A mistake usually just means more adventure, another memory.

So it was in this case. Our only option was to make our way "cross-country" on even smaller roads, slowly moving towards the village of Faux, our ultimate destination. Turns out to be one of the loveliest rides of the trip, biking mile after mile through emerald green pastures in a cool gray mist that hid all but the faded outlines of the farmhouses we passed.

On the fifth day of the tour, we left the relatively flat valley of the Dordogne River with its endless vineyards, and headed up.

Thank goodness for 12-speed bikes. Thank goodness, that is, for gear number one. Forget the other eleven. We shifted into this lowest gear to climb the steep hills leading to Les Eyzies, site of the limestone cliffs that have become an archeological mecca, home of prehistoric man. The hills are hard work for an out-of-shape middle-aged man, but the effort is worth it when we looked back at the breathtaking vistas of the vineyards and farms below with their checkerboard fields of greens, browns and yellows.

"Rest day." That's how the sixth day of the tour was designated on the itinerary, and just in time. There is no heavy bicycling scheduled. Instead, while Julie spies on a French chef, I bike a short distance for a tour of the prehistoric caves, with their fascinating renderings of animals painted in the sandstone walls by Stone Age Man. And Woman, I presume.

In the afternoon, a tournament of round-robin tennis is organized by one of the tour members, using four battered racquets borrowed from the local pharmacist.

The relaxing day is just what the doctor ordered for exhausted muscles.

But what about exhausted stomachs?

After six days of gourmet food and fine wines, my digestive system is begging for a time out.

The first night's oyster-and-caviar appetizer and the entree of "lamproise" (an eel-like delicacy from which an over-indulging Henry I is said to have died) was a bit stressful, sure, but my stomach had put up with it gracefully.

So, too, the five-course Beef Wellington meal on the second night, and the fresh trout with butter lemon sauce (how the French love sauces) on the third night.

But by the fourth night, after the terrine of jellied lotte, the garlic soup, the steamed duck with ginger sauce and the chocolate flan with fresh strawberries, my digestive tract was beginning to wonder when this harassment would end.

And then came the dinner on this fifth day - another five-course extravaganza featuring cream soup, an asparagus-in-pastry full-fledged meal posing as an appetizer, a veal entree too good to be true, a mind-boggling selection of cheeses, and a walnut souffle.

By this time, my stomach was gasping for air.

I staggered away from the table and headed for the room, promising my plumbing system that I absolutely, positively, unequivocally would give it a rest if it would only do its duty this one last time.

The days are beginning to run together, one delightful experience after another, a string of holiday pearls.

Days of lazy bicycling down country lanes, through little clouds of milkweed that dance and swirl in the sun like flakes of snow. Elegant French inns and wondrous overnight accommodations. Sublime picnics along the banks of the Dordogne River. French bread and goat cheese and bottles of cold "grand cru" wine, inexpensively priced. Gourmet dinners every evening.

I lose track of the time.

The seventh day passes, then the eighth and final day of riding.

We have pedaled a total of some 200 miles and in the process come to know our bicycles as "dear friends," just as Sally said we would. It is sad to part.

"Do you suppose," I asked Julie on the final night, as we ate the last chocolate bon bon of our last six-course meal, "that when we're too old to bike we'll still be able to sign up for these tours?

Maybe they'll be willing to just carry us in the van from one hotel to the other, along with all the luggage."

It was a comforting thought.

The wife's first day on the road.

Bordeaux

The Wife's Story

July, 1984

Tim and I are now too old to do the student hike-and-camp tour through Europe and too young to do the Grand Hotels. We want a deeper look into the countryside, the real people, the un-touristy parts of Europe. We want to enjoy all the local specialties of food and wine, but we don't want all those gourmet excesses to grow on our lazily vacationing bodies.

We want to stay in small, charming, out-of-the-way places, but we don't want to share a bathroom with everyone else on the same floor.

Then, voila! An acquaintance mentioned her recent bicycle tour to the south of France. Still glowing, she claimed it was "the best vacation we ever had." Immediately, we put ourselves on the mailing list. That's when we discovered Butterfield & Robinson.

It is early May, and we rendezvous, along with 19 others, at the designated Grand Hotel in Bordeaux, not a hotel but a pristine, modernized chateau that looks like something out of Disney World, set amid manicured gardens and renovated to a bizarre Hollywood '50s style.

Our first room on this trip is carpeted in white, the size of a large Commonwealth Avenue condominium. It has its own separate turret and, in the center of the suite, a round, royal blue bathtub big enough for us to swim laps.

We change to our new biking clothes, and, wondering nervously if the rest of this group has prepared for the trip, physically, the way we have (a few bike excursions to the corner drugstore), we go to meet our bicycles.

They are brand new and each is labeled with one of our names. "We'll try a practice run," say our group leaders, Sally and Peter. "Just over to the nearby abbey and back. It's only seven kilometers."

13

Why should I bother with maps on this little jaunt, I think to myself. I want to enjoy the scenery. Tim can be keeper of the map. I'll just follow him.

This plan works fine on the way over to the abbey. But he tarries on the way back, and I decide that I might as well just bike on ahead, following the road pointed out by Sally.

"Just turn left at the end of the road and follow the group home," she says cheerily. I turn left and pedal along, enjoying the landscape of scrubby vineyards spiked here and there with tall, lanky poplars, and clouds piled like ice cream sundae scoops filling the sky, inspiration for present-day Matisses and Van Goghs.

Suddenly I realize there are no familiar bikers ahead of me. Nor behind me. I am alone. It is late in the afternoon and will soon be dark. I am in chilly little biking shorts and the air has turned cool. A French phrase in the back of our preparatory bicycle book pops into my head: "Mon mari a une tete de bois," or, "My husband has a head of wood (is stubborn)." It seems relevant somehow, but maybe in truth it refers to me. I know how to say "I am lost" in French, but I don't know where I want to be found. Like a three-year-old, I know my name but I don't know where I live. I live in a chateau, but so do a lot of Bordeaux residents. My chateau is in the middle of a huge field, near no town whatsoever.

As I'm wondering why we didn't just rent a car and get lost in France together, I spot, over the crest of a hill, the turrets of our chateau! Like a bullet I backtrack, making right, left, left, right turns down the little roads, watching that yellowed tower draw closer and closer, until, finally, I am home at last, and just in time for a quick swim in the bathtub before dressing for dinner.

We will stay at the same chateau tonight, so today we will take a circular route through the countryside, stopping at two vineyards before we wind back this afternoon to our starting point.

This is the first full day of biking - about 25 miles - and although this leaves time for tasting and meandering, we still seem to be biking for an awfully long time, and our legs are beginning to feel new muscles, or maybe it's old muscles in a new way. Each little uphill feels like an Alp, and my thighs, from the knee to the hip, feel like lead weights. But the peonies, poppies and roses that grow alongside the little roads almost make me forget the sapping of the strength in these aging legs.

We stop in St. Emilion, a beautiful medieval town centered around its most important industry, the wine of the same name. We ride out to two different vineyards and visit with the "vignerons," owners and operators, and discuss with them the quality of their grapes, the pressing and storing of the liquid in its various stages and the ancient rules of wine-growing.

"Red wine goes right to the legs," comments one of our more knowledgeable fellow bikers, and, being female, I naturally think he is talking about calories. He is not. I find that out as soon as I get on my bike. While white wine, it seems, makes bicycling afterward more mellow, red wine makes your legs all wobbly and uncoordinated. I am bicycling just the way I did on my first two-wheeler, only this time my father is not around to steady me. Thank goodness I'm only a menace to myself on these roads, and not to innocent pedestrians.

Our tour notes warn that this day will be the "longest bike ride" of the entire trip. It will be particularly satisfying for the "sportifs," or seriously athletic cyclists of our group." Hmmm, good for them. But what kind of a day, I wonder, will it be for the lazy couch potatoes of the group? Like me and my husband, for example. Theoretically - whether sportif or sedentary - we're all going to the same place, Bergerac, home of Cyrano, an intriguing destination, whatever the ride. Not only are the grapes for Bergerac and Monbazillac wine grown there, but the best truffles in the world are hiding beneath its fertile soil.

Seventy kilometers later: Will these hills never flatten out? Body hurts; knees hurt; they're making clicking noises; seat hurts. I notice husband is starting to stuff sweatshirts over his bicycle seat to help soften the surface. Shoulders hurt. Palms hurt. Fingers tingle and lose sensation.

I slowly get my second wind and feel my energy coming back, but Tim is experiencing real fatigue. I urge him to stay on his bike and keep pedaling, when a big black cloud starts to hover over us. By 6 p.m. we're pedaling in a rainstorm and this, I concede, is a bit much. By magic, the B&R van pulls up just then and carries us bicycles and all, the last few kilometers to our hotel.

On these bike tours, thank goodness, the van takes our suitcases every day from hotel to hotel, leaving us to pedal unencumbered. Each night, when we arrive at our destination, not only are our suitcases already at the hotel, but they are in our rooms. Perhaps we should ask to have our baths drawn and ready, too. On this night, the hot baths felt especially good, and the dinner that followed of fresh trout, Monbazillac white wine and scrambled eggs with truffles was beyond sublime.

A wine tasting in the morning? Only in France.

Right after coffee and croissants, we head for Chateau Monbazillac to taste the sweet sauterne made from Semillon, Sauvignon and Muscadelle grapes. It is drizzling a warm rain, and while this makes cycling unpleasant in the way of squishy shoes and soaked maps, it adds a depth to the already deep green of the

Sharing the road in Bordeaux.

countryside and also to the rich aroma of grape vines, new mown grass, roses, coral bells and barnyard animals.

I have a Gore-Tex hooded jacket, which keeps off most of the rain from the waist up, but many of the more experienced bikers have Gore-Tex long pants as well, and one Southern Californian has had the foresight to pack, in addition, a waterproof biking hat and booties that slip over her shoes to keep them not only dry but warm. She looks like a frogman.

And then we get lost. (This time, at least, husband is with me.) We pedal a difficult, sweaty 10 kilometers up some rolling hills. It's 5:30 in the afternoon and, according to our little map, we have many miles to go before we reach Tremolat. Many more than we knew, it turns out. From a road sign we learn that we are headed toward "Bouniaques" – in the wrong direction.

We adjust our route and set off again, through some of the lushest farmland in the world. We are heading toward Tremolat, along a series of narrow vineyard roads. Cycling along, we think about the five-course dinner that will once again grace our table tonight, assuming we ever find our hotel.

Eventually, thank heaven, we do, and at Tremolat the sun comes out, literally and figuratively. Our hotel, Le Vieux Logis, has been renovated from a chateau and has rooms I have never seen in the best U.S. hotels. Wallpapered in a French provincial print, the room features a half-canopied bed, covered in a reverse print of matching fabric. There is a huge walk-in fireplace and an armchair covered in the same fabric. White carpeting and freshly painted white woodwork, sparkling white lace inner curtains and print draperies set off the antique bedside tables, armoire, desks and writing table.

Knickknacks, obviously old and French, are set around in a casually trusting manner that makes the room look far homier those in the United States.

We all go to our assigned room, all decorated differently, and each of us is sure that we have been awarded the best room of all.

Dinner - which begins with an egg and garlic soup and a terrine of sole, lotte, turbot and vegetables - continues along the same vein to steamed duckling, tarragon-covered goat- cheese balls and a dessert tray filled with a dozen kinds of sweets. It is taken in charmingly renovated stables, with high tiny-paned windows, fabric-covered round tables and fresh flowers in brass pots.

We awake in total darkness. Is it midnight? No, it's morning but the Bordeaux innkeepers actually go around the inn each night and shut the outside shutters. We have been enclosed and protected from dangers and daylight.

The high hills on our route today are more than offset by the spectacular scenery.

Picture the colors of fields full of lupen (royal blue), wild daisies (white), Oriental poppies (red), thistle (lavender) and buttercups (yellow) set among chateaus rising above the Dordogne River, cows grazing around it all.

We have to get off our bicycles and walk up the "heartbreak hills," not regretting the slower pace, because this allows us to see more of the wildflowers.

The big downhill ride takes us into the delightful town of Limeuil, set at the confluence of the Dordogne and Vezere rivers.

It is time for a "pique-nique." All the stores close for two hours at noon, and since it is 11:45 a.m., we rush to the boulangerie and charcuterie for French bread, local cheese, wine. We ask for a bottle of white wine and the clerk tells us we can buy vin ordinaire for 80 cents per bottle. No, we say munificently, we'd like a bottle of your best dry white Bordeaux. "If you want to spend that kind of money," she implies, "you can buy this" - the best white wine of Bordeaux, for $1.80.

Giving thanks for an accident-free day

The afternoon ride is one of the most enjoyable yet. The route is not as hilly or long as in previous days, so we are not pushing ourselves to get to the destination of Les Eyzies. There is no traffic on the little road, so it looks like our own private bicycle path through this lush farmland. Best of all, we are not lost.

About 3 p.m. we cross a bridge and come into Les Eyzies to find the Hotel Les Glycines, our flower- bedecked home for the next two nights. Its front terrace, roofed in grapevines, is laden with pots of daisies, primroses and pansies, and across the street is a little stone house with a garden that looks like a French Impressionist painting - tall purple iris mixed in with smaller purple lupens and pink and purple columbine. There are more flowers in this little town than at the Boston Flower Show.

We visit the museum of prehistory, which has put this town on the map as a center of Cro-Magnon Man artifacts, and stop on the way back at a tavern for currant sherbet, which served as a palate cleanser for what was to come that evening at the hotel: Soup Julienne Darblay, with tiny julienned vegetables in a consomme; white asparagus in a delicate puff pastry and cream sauce; paper-thin slices of braised veal; creamed spinach and miniature vegetables placed on the side of the plate (a touch of red cabbage and one perfect, tiny carrot) as an art form - all taken that day from the chef's garden that adjoins the hotel. Husband nearly keeled over when the meal continues with a chevres cheese from this region, and walnut souffles, baked for precisely 20 minutes and brushed with sugar. The red wine, incidentally, was a Societe d'Experience du Chateau de Terigand. The white was a Chateau Panisseau Bergerac Sec. The water? It wasn't vintage; it was plain old mineral.

Not surprisingly, both of us dreamt about food last night, I of roast suckling pig; Tim of a roast turkey or goose, he is not sure which.

We have a free day today, with no biking scheduled, so some will go to the nearby caves to see the paintings of prehistoric man that still remain there. I will follow the chef around on his daily routine, at his gracious invitation, to try to learn some of his secrets.

The day is lazy and beautiful, with tennis played on a local court before a sudden shower forces us once again to the dinner table and yet another meal. You know the drill: consommé, terrines of trout and salmon, roast lamb in truffle sauce, mousse of fresh vegetables, cheeses and strawberries in melted ice cream. With it, a red Chateau Haut Brion St. Emilion, 1970, and a white Cheval Blanc St. Emilion 1970. Is there life after Bordeaux?

We are getting dissolute; we have discovered that, if you place your order for breakfast the night before, it is brought to your bedroom. Therefore, breakfast this morning - orange juice, coffee, chocolate croissants, thin homemade toast and two kinds of homemade jam - is taken "en chambre."

About 9:30 a.m., we begin biking past limestone cliffs and dewy farmland with poppies growing wild in the fields. A farm machine is cutting and churning up field grass, and along with it, thousands of poppies, which in the middle of New York City could probably command $5 per bloom. Nearly every tiny town we come to today is dominated by a huge fortress built into the top of a hill. The fortresses are constructed from the same material as the cliffs, and are the same color. They look like they were hand-carved, with their towers and gargoyles and glass windows.

We are back along the Dordogne River, and the roads are fairly flat except for the one huge hill that must be crossed in order to get to our day's destination, Sarlat. Up and up and up. I don't try to bike it, even in my lowest gear. Just get off and walk, with my calves crying for mercy, my lungs gasping for this sweet air. The sun is beating down and it is hot, but like New England, wait a minute. The clouds gather suddenly, and it rains, ever so slightly on us. A tropical little shower nearly every day, with sunshine afterward to dry us off.

We are lost again, but only slightly. There are a number of routes over this hill, and all will eventually lead to Sarlat. We've been getting more adventurous and trying our own individual routes. The beauty of these loosely structured tours is that everyone can bicycle together as a group, and sometimes do, or can split into smaller groups, depending on desired speed. More often than not, husband and I prefer bicycling alone, free to meditate and soak in the scenery, with no noise except the call of cuckoo birds. Typically, the back roads we travel have very few cars

We arrive in Sarlat about 4 p.m. at the Hotel de la Madeleine, and I take note of my amazing ability on this trip to fall asleep anywhere, immediately, as soon as I become prone, with my running shoes still on. Heavenly sleep until dinner: a salad of walnuts, avocado, tongue and tomato; goose liver on toast in a rich gravy; roast duck; chocolate tarts, washed down with a white table wine of the region called La Tassel du Patron.

The last day of biking. My right leg now shows the classic signs of the biker: the bruises from knee to toe where I've pedaled carelessly and my foot has slipped. But counteracting these battle wounds, my legs are also now tanned and strong; where once there was dough for a thigh, now I think I can detect an ever-so-slight curve of real muscle. For a few hours more, I can feel like a real jock. In front of my hotel, before I get on my bike, I bend and stretch my new leg muscles as if I'm in training for one of the heavy-duty cross country bike races they hold here. Passers-by will never know that I'm going to hop off this bike as soon as I get around the corner and walk up the first hill 200 meters from here.

The afternoon is spent moving along leisurely through the countryside, past the ripening walnut trees and the castles, one after another, set majestically on the highest hill of each town. About 5 p.m., we arrive at our final lodging, a 14th-century castle overlooking the Dordogne on 300 acres of formal gardens. It is our private chateau; we own it just for this one lovely spring night in France, and we will have a private party to end all parties.

Everyone's room has a brass plate on the door with a different name. Our room, three flights of stone stairs and then another tiny half flight up to the very top of the chateau, is called the Prison Room. The two tiny windows bordered by a cozy window seat, are barred. The ceilings are about 20 feet high. The bedspread is real fur. The walls are stone, and the bathtub is set into a stone block as though it were a natural pool.

We feel, as we sit at the garret nibbling on the fresh strawberries that were waiting in a tiny bowl by the window seat, like a princess and a knight banished from society, but not too worried about the prospect of staying around here for the next hundred years or so.

Our biking group, strangers a week ago, now united in a nine-day bond of special experiences, gathers as old friends for a dinner that begins with a punchbowl full of Kir Royale (champagne and cassis), our official French cocktail hour drink, and trays of caviar.

A pianist has been called in to play for our private dinner, and we hear, for the first time in nine days, American jazz and swing. It is wonderful music to American ears. In my opinion, the only thing the French don't do as well as the Americans is popular music. The after-dinner champagne and the music makes everyone feel like dancing, and before long my husband — normally the world's most reticent man on the dance floor - is so carried away with the festivities that he asks the delighted chateau keeper for a turn around the stone floor.

The beauty of the trip is that each of us will remember our trip differently. The two beer-loving couples from Vancouver who bicycled from cafe to cafe will remember the trip for its brews. The woman from Ohio will remember the churches she visited. Bill from California will remember it for the challenge to his leg muscles. A few of us will remember it for its flowers and its first-course terrines. John, the horse breeder from Kentucky, will remember it for the French stud farms. Sumner, from Maine, will remember it for the wines, and his wife Helen will remember it for the birds. Don the New Yorker, a self-confessed workaholic at home, will remember it for the peace and quiet and respite from all responsibility. "I must have died and gone to Heaven," he was heard to mutter one afternoon as he biked along a narrow flower-bordered lane.

We all felt the same way.

MILAN TO VENICE

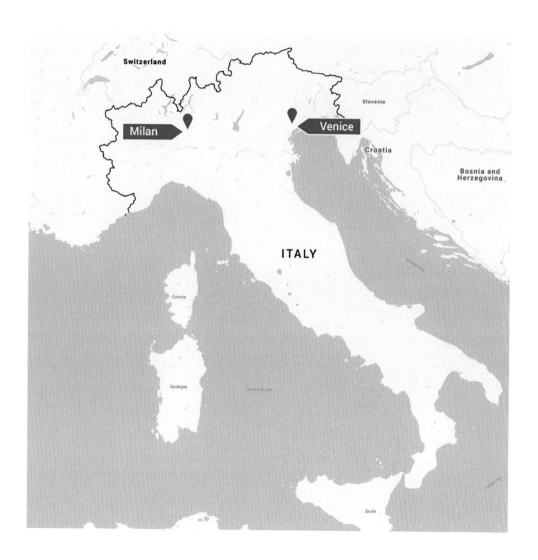

Picnics on biking tours are three-course meals.

Milan to Venice

July, 1986

Life on the fast track.

That was what we wanted when we signed up for another bicycle tour in Europe. A little adventure, a little danger. Life on the edge.

Last year it was a leisurely bike tour through the wine country of Bordeaux. Kid stuff. The only injury suffered on that trip was a tiny scrape on the back of Julie's ankle when her foot slipped off the pedal as we braked to a stop for a midafternoon wine tasting.

This year we would put ourselves in harm's way.

This year we would take a luxury bike trip from Milan to Venice.

The dangers were everywhere. And they increased with every passing week after we sent in our deposit for the trip.

First came the U.S. raid on Libya in retaliation for the bombing of the German nightclub.

We knew what that meant: There would probably be a terrorist in every other plane flying to Europe this summer, and American tourists walking through the terminals or hotel lobbies abroad would be risking life and limb. Italy was mentioned as especially hazardous.

"Let's chance it," we said. "We'll stay out of hotel lobbies."

Then came the northern Italian wine scandal. Someone was lacing cheap Italian wine with methanol.

"Let's go anyway," we said. "We'll only drink expensive wine."

Then came the nuclear meltdown at Chernobyl. The TV newscasts showed ominous radiation clouds drifting southward over the Alps, spilling their lethal residue on the slopes of northern Italy. We knew what that meant: The milk and cheese would all be irradiated, a ticking time bomb for pregnant mothers.

"Perfect," we said. "We won't have any more children." (One of our close relatives began pressuring us about the children that we did have, wondering out loud in front of us what would become of them if...)

Finally came news of the serial killer in northern Italy, as reported in Time magazine. Every summer since 1981, "the Monster of Florence," in Time's words, has been using distinctive copper-jacketed Winchester bullets to knock off couples camping in the Italian countryside.

"No problem," we said. "We'll sleep indoors."

And so we went.

Traveling in Europe this year was a little out of the ordinary, no doubt about it.

We knew it was going to be different when Alitalia canceled our flight from Boston to Milan two days before we were to depart.

"Not enough passengers to make it worthwhile," the travel agent explained. "We'll have to find another carrier."

Waiting in line at the New York check-in counter of Pan Am two days later, we studied the other passengers with suspicion. They all looked like terrorists.

And as we filled out Pan Am identification tags for our luggage, we paused, wondering whether putting something so American on our bags was a good idea.

After a moment's reflection, the offending little tags were ripped off, crumpled up and thrown away. When you're going on a dangerous mission you can't be too careful.

On our first day in Milan before our bike trip began, in the crowds of shoppers that swirled down the Via Monte Napoleone and Via della Spiga, we didn't see a single pair of Bermuda shorts. No plaid sport coats, either. No penny loafers. Not even any Reeboks.

In short, there wasn't an American in sight. Except us - but we were traveling incognito, wearing the clothes we thought looked least American in our wardrobes.

For Tim, that meant white sailor pants with a string tie-belt and a green windbreaker tucked in at the waist - the perfect disguise, he thought.

"You look like some ridiculous cross between an AWOL Coast Guard cadet and a vagabond Dutch student," said Julie. She said it in Italian, so that no one would know she was American. No matter that Tim did not speak Italian. It seemed judicious to have at least one of us speaking in the native tongue, if only to herself.

The next afternoon, we met our Butterfield & Robinson tour group (16 persons in all) at the beautiful walled town of Sermione on Lake Garda for the official start of our journey through "the villas and vineyards of Northern Italy."

There are no billboards en route to Venice.

As always on these trips, the first order of business was to introduce ourselves to the bicycles that B&R provided us – in this case, brand new machines, sleek and shiny– and take a short spin through the surrounding countryside. The bikes have an opportunity to introduce themselves to *us*, as well, and it always takes awhile before each is comfortable with the other.

We were put up that night at the Villa Cortine, former summer residence of the British ambassador to Italy. It is a stunningly beautiful mansion situated in the center of a private park on the edge of the lake. A chilled bottle of champagne, courtesy of B&R, waited for us in our room.

After a swim in the heated pool and a walk in the garden, we dined that evening on a meal of antipasto of mussels, squid and shrimp; spaghetti with wild mushrooms in a cream sauce; veal piccata; fresh broiled fish; and profiteroles. All paired with quantities of a vintage red Bardolino.

Sure, it tasted good, but Tim was taking precautions, nevertheless. "The Chernobyl fallout is serious," he declared. "I'm not going to eat any milk products." That meant no milk in his coffee. When the cheeses came around, he dutifully chose only the hard varieties, on the supposition that radiation can more easily penetrate the soft ones.

But by the fourth course (and second bottle of wine), the sharp edge of the constant danger under which we were living seemed to have receded. He fearlessly accepted a slice of buffalo mozzarella. He had come 4,000 miles from Boston and there was no radiation in sight. Perhaps we would get through this after all.

The next morning, however, we discovered we were not out of trouble.

It had been raining for several days in the mountains to the north of us, and this, we were told, had pushed cesium from the Chernobyl radiation cloud into the Lake Garda area, right where we were. Who knew what cesium was, let alone what it did to the human body, but anything with an "i-u-m" at the end of it in these nuclear-powered days strikes terror to the heart. Strangely, all the Italians around us seemed to go on about their business that morning as if they had no cesium filtering through their systems.

For us, living on the edge, this would require special action. That evening, after pedaling the 28-mile route along the western shore of the lake, through the lowlands of Lugano, past the vineyards of Riviera del Garda, through the pretty town of Salo (where Bertolotti de Salo, inventor of the violin, was born) to the Grand Hotel in Gardone Riviera, where we stopped for the night, Tim took more precautions. He decided then and there to avoid all fresh fruit.

Well, at least to peel it. After the five-course meal, enhanced by a red Valpolicella and a white Colli Albani, he carefully peeled off the skins of his fresh peaches and apricots, avoiding any possible contamination on them from the rain. He allowed himself a cup of cappuccino, which has milk in it, of course, but he had no choice. It was already there so maybe it wasn't dangerous, he thought, as he sipped the delicious brew.

The very next day brought new hazards.

Our biking schedule - a 31-mile jaunt from Gardone Riviera to the splendid old town of Verona - included a midmorning visit to a roadside "enoteca," the local establishments in Italy dedicated to the tasting of regional wines.

Would this expose us to the wines of northern Italy that had been so much in the news lately? The ones adulterated with methanol? Once again we knew we were flirting with danger - but hey that's the kind of vacation we wanted, right? Once again we decided to risk it.

The enoteca took place outdoors around a large oaken table on a cool patio enshrouded by vines that protected against the summer sun. Sipping from delicate tulip-stemmed glasses that glistened in the light, we tasted and tested some of the best wines of Italy - proceeding from a 1984 Lugana, to a 1982 Soave, to a 1981 Valpolicella Classico, to a 1983 Bardolino, to a 1978 Recioto

Amarone (Dio mio!), a wine so exceptional that the Italians don't bottle it every year, only in the years when they feel it will be perfect.

Somewhere between the Soave '82 and the Valpolicella '81, our worries of going blind from methanol began to recede. When the last drop of Amarone was gone, we got back on our bikes and weaved down the road - or what looked like the road - toward Verona. It's true we weren't seeing quite as well as before, but we weren't worried anymore.

"Courage has its own rewards," said Julie.

Each morning on a B & R bicycle tour, the two guides give you a page of directions to that night's destination and trace the route on your map before sending you on your way. Then they put your luggage in a van and have it waiting for you in your room when you arrive later that afternoon.

On the fourth day of our trip, leaving Verona behind (but not the echoes of the Palestrina motets sung antiphonally in the ancient church by the University of Verona choral students the night before), we set off for Montagnana, 26 miles away.

It was a soft summer morning. We pedaled along through sweeping stretches of vineyards, up and down the gently rolling hills, past the green-and-yellow fields where farmers were planting hundreds of flowering roses to keep out pests that attacked their grapevines.

We were in the hinterlands of northern Italy, home of the maniacal "Monster of Florence." His bullet, they say, often kills both the man and woman with one shot. He has a particular predilection for couples in rural settings like the one in which we were biking. He could be anywhere.

Was it the little man in the black suit who followed Julie up the hill, pedaling furiously on his rickety old bike with the balloon tires? He carried a black satchel that looked very much like a gun case.

Was it the seemingly nice old lady in the house beside the road (the one with all the roses), who came out with a bicycle pump and tried to help us fix our flat tire? Anything's possible.

Was it the man in the blue pickup truck, parked beside the field of red poppies, who drew us a map on a piece of scrap paper when we missed the turn to Gazzola? He had a strange lop-sided smile.

They all looked suspicious. And they all sounded suspicious, too. Every one of them spoke Italian, the native tongue of the killer.

None of them, as it turned out, laid a finger on us. But as our bike tour neared its end, a new and insidious danger - one of the most serious yet - unexpectedly emerged.

Rose bushes stand guard against insects in Italian vineyards.

Every day that we had increased our biking efforts to burn away the extra calories acquired during the trip, B&R had increased the quantity and quality of our meals. We began to feel, in the pits of our groaning stomachs, the grim possibility of massive gastro-intestinal failure.

We had consumed great mounds of delicate risotto and pasta, cooked with butter and garlic and artichoke paste and even vodka sauce. We had savored tender veal cooked alla marsala, al limone, al pomodoro. We had indulged ourselves over and again with "tiramisu," the degenerate chocolate-and-cream Italian dessert that translates roughly to: "pick me up from under the table after I eat this."

Then, on the sixth day, between the Michelin-starred dinner in Rubano and the six-course banquet in Zerman, we had what B&R modestly referred to as a "group picnic by the wayside."

It was spread out on white tablecloths, festooned with wildflowers, when we pedaled up the hill to the appointed spot. There, on the grass, under a shade tree looking out over the green-carpeted Po Valley, we helped ourselves to:

Dishes of cold vitello tonnato, tender slices of marinated eggplant, three kinds of bread baked earlier that morning, marinated wild mushrooms, paper-thin prosciutto, huge slices of dripping-ripe tomatoes with burrata cheese and capers in olive oil (yes, buratta is a soft cheese, and, yes, Tim helped himself to a large hunk, but he figured he had already mistakenly eaten some Bel Paese the day before and had not died from it, so what the heck?), Swiss cheese, spiced ham, hard salami, olives and, for dessert, fresh cherries, peaches, oranges, strawberries and an Italian cake full of almonds. This was accompanied by quantities of cold spumante or beer and topped off with an ice cream cone from "the best gelato shop in Italy" up the road.

Our stomachs were still not off the hook that day.

Five hours later, at our next hotel, we had a "rustic country dinner" that began with prosciutto mantagna on cantaloupe and continued with fagottino al tonno (baked pastry with tuna inside), spaghetti carbonara, stinco de maiale (pork), scaloppa al limone, piselli al prosciutto, and pomodori gratinati, ending with a dessert of Italian ice cream with a meringue filling. Julie bet that there was no meringue inside, so Tim had to order a second helping to prove it to her.

The next morning we both lay in bed, silently staring at the ceiling for several moments after the alarm sounded.

"I can't move," Julie said, finally. "I think I have gout."

Our last full day of bicycling was also our longest - a total of 33 miles from Rubano to Venice.

We had faced every threat and every danger in this land of peril without flinching, taking our chances at every turn.

Now, as we rode through the old villages of the Veneto, along the peaceful edge of the Brenta Canal, down narrow winding roads, through fields of wildflowers... the fears of traveling abroad this summer were fading.

The day was overcast. The air was sweet and still, heavy with the fragrance of roses, at their seasonal peak on this particular week of early June. Every house and farm, no matter how small, seemed to have its rose garden, in spectacular bloom.

From time to time, we bicycled past elegant old villas, witness to an earlier era, aging gracefully, proud and silent.

In the 15th and 16th centuries, these magnificent buildings with their stunning ornamental statuary and elaborate gardens (some with ingenious hedge mazes that still confuse modern-day visitors) were homes for the aristocracy.

We stopped for lunch in the little town of Mira. Lord Byron had been there before us. In 1817. His house, with a tiny placard on the front, was next to the cafe where we went for fried squid and a cold beer.

Late in the afternoon, as we neared Venice - our final destination - we stopped one last time for another Italian ice cream cone, selecting, one scoop of amaretto and another of light green kiwi from the many delectable alternatives.

That night, after bidding farewell to the other bikers, as we ate dinner by ourselves in our little Venice pensione overlooking the Grand Canal, we raised our glass of Montepulciano to the dangers of European travel in the summer of 1986, recalling the words of the Italian taxi driver who had driven us into Milan from the airport.

Don't sweat it, he had advised, speaking of the perils of travel. "Si puo vivere un giorno come un lione, oppuve cento giorni come una pecora."

"You can live one day like a lion," he noted, "or a hundred days like a lamb."

PROVENCE, FRANCE

When dining in Provence, expect surprises.

Provence

August, 1987

"You want to go back to *France?*" the husband asked, incredulously. "You want to go back again? We've been to France once. We've done France." He was referring to a bike trip two years earlier. "Provence isn't France," the wife replied superciliously. "It's different. It's a whole new country."

And so we went back to France, to Provence, for our third luxury bike trip to Europe in three years.

Since taking that first spin on wheels, we've become addicted to this particular form of European transportation - and the kind of tour package that goes with it.

Similar packages are now offered by a number of travel companies: Choose your country (France, England, Germany, Scotland, etc.), pay your money in advance, and show up when and where the tour begins. You'll receive a gleaming 12-speed bike, a map, some daily directions giving your intended route, and the tender loving care of knowledgeable young guides, who will take all your luggage ahead in a van every day to the next chateau, castle or inn where you'll be staying that evening.

The rest is up to you. It's merely a matter of making your legs move, pedaling leisurely through the countryside - smelling the flowers, tasting the wine, listening to the birds, feeling the sun on your back, finding your way down little lanes and country byways to the next fabulous meal at the end of the day.

The husband had made one more effort to shift their sights away from France this year. "Why don't we try Hungary?" he asked, plaintively. "It might be very interesting."

"Hungary-Shmungary," the wife retorted. "Let's go for the gold. Provence will knock your socks off."

And she was right.

Arriving in Paris, we raced down to Avignon in one of the country's high-speed "bullet" trains. Within the walls of that ancient city, home of the French papacy between 1305 and 1377, we met our tour group - 24 in all, hailing from all corners of the United States and Canada, young and old, couples and singles, athletes and non-athletes, the diverse group of folks typically found on these kinds of trips.

That night, after introductions at dinner, the group slept in the 14th-century chateau of Rochegude, which, like most of our accommodations on the trip, was a member of "Relais et Chateaux," France's most distinguished chain of inns and hotels, noted for their beauty, historic significance and superior food and service. (The tour was sponsored by Butterfield & Robinson of Toronto, a company that promises the best of everything.)

The next morning - each of us with a state-of-the-art bike carefully adjusted to our individual specifications - we set out for our first day of biking.

"It seems the same as Bordeaux to me," said the husband, coasting down the little road that led away from the chateau. "This is just like our other trip to France."

But almost immediately, even to the husband, the contrasts between the regions began to reveal themselves.

To begin with, the Provence countryside actually looks quite different. The vineyards went on for miles, and the grape vines themselves were thicker and stubbier, with their trunks hunkered close to the ground.

The fragrances of Provence are different too. When we were in Bordeaux, the smells were heavy and wet - the rich smell of newly-turned earth; the sweetly pungent smell of manure; the sharp smell of freshly-mowed grass.

In Provence, the smells are drier, lighter, sunnier: the delicate scent of lavender, the redolent fragrance of Scotch broom, musky smells of fields baking in the sun, the perfume of thyme, rosemary and wildflowers that fills the air.

Speaking of flowers, there seem to be even more varieties of wildflowers in Provence (is it possible?) than in Bordeaux: great pools of orange poppies shimmer in the sun, fields of bright yellow broom, sprigs of delicate pink, purple and blue "weeds" growing beside the road.

One of these flowers, a light but intensely colored bluebell, is said to have inspired the color of blue denim, and we recalled as we biked a few kilometers from the town of Nimes that here was where the original fabric and its name "denim" (a contraction of "de Nimes") began.

Then there are the hills. Provence has more of them than Bordeaux. They're gentle, but they seem to go on forever, especially if you're out of shape and you're on a bicycle and you're pedaling to the top of one. Could it be mathematically possible, we wondered occasionally, for Provence to have more up hills than down hills?

Thankfully, there was always an exquisite chateau or castle awaiting us for the night at the top of the day's final uphill push as a reward.

There is more sun in Provence, too. The hot sun is good for grapes, they say - but who wants to be a grape in the middle of the day when you're riding a bike? Biking in Bordeaux, by and large, is cooler and more comfortable. It can also be considerably wetter. In Provence, we didn't have a single day of rain.

The incredible sunlight of Provence is what, for so many years, has drawn artists from all over the world to set up their easels here.

"Why does that scene look so familiar?" we asked ourselves, cycling between St. Remy and Arles, struck by a particularly beautiful clump of sunflowers in front of a vineyard stretching out to a distant, tall stand of swaying poplar trees, a little house with a red tile roof nearby and a sharp cotton ball of a cloud in an intensely blue sky above.

The answer was that we had seen it before. In Boston's Museum of Fine Arts, among other art museums. This is Van Gogh country. These were the very scenes he painted while living in Provence.

A tiny, sad bust of the artist, already shorn of his right ear, now sits near a brick wall on the grounds of the St. Remy mental hospital where he died so tragically. And St. Remy residents, some of whom talk as if they feel personally responsible for the town's ostracizing of the artist back in the late 1800s, note apologetically that there is not one original Van Gogh painting left within the town's perimeters.

If Provence has more sun than Bordeaux, it also, on occasion, has more wind. A lot more.

This is the infamous Provencal "mistral," an insistent wind that funnels down the Rhone Valley from the Alps to Provence. If you're unlucky, it can be in your face for days at a time. In our case, it buffeted our bicycles on the road for a few short hours one afternoon and then - as mysteriously as it appeared - blew away.

Even the husband knew from the beginning about one aspect of Provence that distinguishes it from the rest of France - its cuisine.

The tomato, the garlic and the olive are the building blocks of Provencal cooking, which traces its roots to the Latin influence of Roman occupation, BC.

On the first night of the tour, therefore, when we sat down to the opening Michelin-starred dinner, we were looking forward to the bouillabaisse, ratatouille (made with fresh Provencal tomatoes) and other specialties that are part of this famous cuisine.

But none of it was in sight.

Instead, we gorged ourselves on truffle-stuffed pasta in consommé, salmon mousse with spinach puree, noisettes of lamb nouvelle, pate of foix gras in warmed salad, a cheese plate of endless variety and a frozen nougat dessert in a vanilla sauce.

"What a disappointment that was," the husband said at the end of the meal, lapping up the last of the vanilla sauce. "Where are the tomatoes?"

The next four days brought more of the same, as the chefs on the tour alternated between exquisite concoctions of traditional Parisienne fare on the one hand and elaborate presentations of magnificent 'nouvelle cuisine' on the other. We had to plow our way through filets of beef in zucchini puree, mousselines of trout, poached salmon in butter sauce, fillets of native fish in mustard sauce, quantities of fresh cheese, together with "chariots" of patisserie (as the menu always put it) that rolled by in a never-ending procession of mind-boggling sweets.

On the fifth day, after a six-course B&R dinner featuring three different cream sauces, we rebelled. The next day we went looking for a true Provencal meal on our own - finding it for lunch, at last, in a little roadside bistro overlooking a 15th- century castle on the Rhone.

It began with a bucketful of "tellines," fingernail-sized clams drenched in garlic sauce that, when spooned into a bowl, sounded like pebbles falling into a child's pail at the beach. Next came a platter of thickly sliced tomatoes in olive oil, sprinkled with fresh parsley.

The entree was a succulent whole roast quail, served on the platter with everything except its feathers intact, including head and feet.

Delicious as it was, the husband carved into it a little cautiously, wondering whether his lifelong membership in the Audubon Society would be canceled if word leaked out.

A few other notes on the Provence eating-drinking-biking experience:

The most famous wine of Provence, the Chateauneuf-du-Pape, is deservedly called "King of the Rhone," and while it doesn't seem to have quite the stature of the great Bordeaux reds, it went down very easily at the roadside establishments for "degustations," otherwise know as wine tastings.

While we had experienced planned tastings at various chateaus in Bordeaux, it was in Provence that we were able to stop our bicycles at a roadside self-serve booth, like an American farm stand, and help ourselves to a taste of the local grower's wine, with stemmed wine glasses set out for visitors. Those who liked it well enough rang for the owner to come out and sell them a few bottles of the same vintage.

The cherry trees were in full fruit when we were there, and bicycling underneath the branches laden with dark red cherries, we couldn't resist picking some along the way, reachable just above our heads. They were incredibly sweet, and so ripe the juice dribbled down our chins as we rolled along.

As for those Provence olives we were lucky enough, thanks to a friend in the French Consulate's office in Boston, to spend an afternoon with one of the region's major olive growers - her uncle, Monsieur Bernard Ducru - whose lovely old estate sat amid his 2,000-year-old olive trees near the town of Mausanne.

"These olive trees produce the best olive oil in the world," he boasted during the delightful lunch al fresco beside the groves. Ducru served us olive bread with homemade tapenade, eggs mimosa and perfectly roasted lamb, followed by

Biking isn't the only mode of transportation on these tours.

raspberry meringue sorbet cake soaked with fresh cherry sauce. "The reason the trees produce such perfect olives is God's secret," he noted. "I have little to do with it." We asked him how a tree that lived in Christ's time could still be around today. "Olive trees, constantly rejuvenate themselves from the center of the tree," he explained. "They do that generation after generation."

In addition to ancient olive trees, Provence has numerous archaeological ruins scattered about the countryside, and the next day we found ourselves in B&R kayaks instead of on bikes in order to see one of the most historic of them: the "Pont du Gard," a 2,000-year-old Roman aqueduct that remains one of the architectural wonders of the world. (In Bordeaux we had explored equally interesting ruins of a different epoch, the Cro-Magnon caves near Les Eyzies,)

While most of our fellow cyclists found that a kayak in white water is like a bicycle without brakes on a downhill grade, they agreed that the multiple drenchings were well worth the spectacular views on this particular excursion. We paddled four miles down the River Gard to view the imposing three-tiered structure from water level, a spectacular sight - and not the only one. Around each bend in the river we drifted past scenes that made the Folies Bergere look like a nunnery. Women in Provence, it turns out, love to lounge like lizards on these hot riverside rocks, totally in the nude. (Even the very pregnant ones.)

"We certainly didn't see anything like that in Bordeaux," the wife noted smugly as she paddled to the landing. "Will you admit now that Provence is worth a separate the trip to France?"

The husband did admit it. "You were right," he conceded. "Provence is different."

Notwithstanding these differences, however, European bike tours all have certain similarities no matter where one goes.

Each of them is like an adult treasure hunt. Every morning, tour members receive a set of directions to that evening's lodging, along with notes about special points of interest along the way.

Given the diminutive back-country roads and primitive signage, following these directions can be quite a challenge. Sample:

"At the main square in town with the fountain of the little boy peeing, bear soft right toward the boulevard Cavaillon, not the sharp right that takes you toward Arles. Look for a small white sign 'Route de vins' and go left around the sign; a small pond at the bottom of a medium sized hill will alert you to the left turn. There are two different 'C-18' routes right here; be sure you take the left or you'll end up at a dead end after 18 beautiful but unnecessary kilometers.

That route will also introduce you to a larger, steeper, hill that will not make you happy. After you see a small red post on the right side of the road, you

In Provence, the delicate scent of lavender perfumes the air.

should be facing a gravel road, slightly bumpy, which lasts for 4 kilometers until you see a white farmhouse and a field of cows. Make a gradual right turn after the farmhouse and soon you should be crossing a little wood bridge over a dry riverbed; don't look for water in the river. If you see water, you're at the wrong bridge."

Lack of fluency in the native tongue doesn't help either. At any given time, you may find yourself digging deep into your limited reserve of French to construct a question such as: "Monsieur, is there a bell tower near here with an orange sign next to an intersection that points the way to the Gasteau Winery?"

But, assuming you are able to follow directions reasonably well and never give up, you always come at the end of the day to a hot bath, chilled champagne, clean sheets and a gourmet meal.

Even if you don't follow directions you'll get there eventually, thanks to a B&R van that will come out looking for you late in the afternoon if you haven't arrived at the destination.

Either way, you'll almost certainly have memorable experiences along the way. "You can't take the wrong route on this trip," our Butterfield & Robinson guide noted at the start of the tour. "Any road you take will be an adventure."

On every one of these European bike tours, whatever the country, there comes a moment of pure joy, a particular time on a particular day during which the bicyclist feels inexplicable exhilaration, a momentary period of exuberance and contentment beyond all measure, when everything comes together in perfect place: the day, the mood, the scenery, the solitude.

Surfboarders search for the perfect wave. Bicyclists search for the perfect road.

In Provence, the moment came on a dirt lane between Tarascon and St. Etienne-du-Gre. Wildflowers shimmered in the fields on either side and swallows darted about in the sunlight overhead as we biked quietly through the countryside, alone with our thoughts, the fragrance of wild roses wafting about us in the soft summer air.

Our last night's stay was in the restored 12th-century Abbaye St. Croix, located on a mountaintop looking toward Marseilles and the Mediterranean.

Its dining room was the former chapel, eerily beautiful with the last rays of sunlight hitting its two-story stone walls. The medieval scene inspired our little tour group to make use of the spiritual accoutics of the place. Standing around a long oak table set with blue and white crockery and long-stemmed wine glasses for our final meal together, we all sang, monk-style, a quickly rehearsed four-part Doxology as a pre-dinner grace.

AUSTRIA & HUNGARY

A Hungarian serenade al fresco.

Austria & Hungary

September, 1989[1]

It was the pig, roasting on a spit in a small alcove off the dark passageway as we descended the stone steps of the 13th-century castle. That's what did it.

The castle was gloomy and forbidding, especially so only one day out of Boston, an abrupt step back through time in this age of air travel.

This was our first night's accommodation, a castle-turned-hotel in Lockenhaus, Austria, complete with its very own torture chamber, the starting point of our bike trip through the territory of the old Hapsburg Empire.

The torture chamber was equipped much the way it had been in the Middle Ages when the castle was used by Knights of the Templar to protect the region from Mongol invaders. It still contained the same "Iron Maiden" employed back then, a monstrous contraption laced with iron spikes that perforated anyone unfortunate enough to be inside when the door was closed.

But it was the pig roasting over the orange coals at the top of the stone stairs leading down into the castle's pitch-black banquet hall (where we ate like the knights of yore with our fingers, even the tossed salad) - it was the whole pig on the spit, head and all, that suddenly gave us the sense of a totally different world.

This was not southern France nor northern Italy, where we had recently biked. This was going to be altogether new. And that was fine, because it was why we had come. The program was the same: We had shiny, multi-gear bikes, daily maps showing the location of the next night's accommodation and a van with guides who transported our luggage from one spot to the next.

---

[1] *In 1989, when this article was published, Hungary was still behind the Iron Curtain.*

45

The rest was up to us. Which means making our legs move all day, every day, with frequent stops for smelling the flowers, photographing the ruins and, of course, drinking the wine.

Speaking of which, let's be up front on one thing at the very start: The wine of Austria is eminently forgettable. That's our opinion at least.

On the other hand, the beer in Hungary and Austria beats anything in France and Italy by a country mile.

Sit down at a cafe on a hot summer day in the ancient center of Sopron and order a chilled glass of golden Schwechater Bier (by sign language, if necessary), and it will make you wonder what they know about malt fermentation that we don't.

And if the beer is especially good for thirsty bikers in Austria and Hungary, so are the roads. Unlike parts of northern Italy, where increasing traffic can sometimes be a problem, the roads in these two countries are ideal for biking - quiet little byways through lovely green farmland, where you can pedal along for a half-hour or more without seeing a car.

Over the years, we have gradually outfitted ourselves with ever more sophisticated paraphernalia to travel on two wheels these byways in distant lands.

We're not talking professional bikers here, understand. Like most of the armchair athletes who take these trips, the closest this middle-aged couple comes to bicycles during the rest of the year is the stationary exercise bikes at our local health club. Hey, let's face it, we're over-weight and under-conditioned. But appearance is the key to road respect when it comes to biking, so we've gradually acquired an assortment of hot-shot apparel.

Where the husband once sat on a rolled-up sweatshirt to cushion his aching backsides on the first trip to Bordeaux, he now brings his very own softly padded seat cover ($28) to place under his softly padded bicycle pants ($31.95).

Where the wife went gloveless in Provence and wore a little knitted scarf around her head, she now wears special leather-lined riding gloves ($18) and sports a dashing red-and-white biking cap with turned-up brim ($5). The husband, who also has a biker's hat, went one step further this trip, investing in a spiffy white biker's helmet ($60).

"You look like a giant mushroom," the wife said disparagingly the first time he put the polyurethane contraption on. (He had to admit it was true, but it gave him a sense of entitlement as he threaded his way through village traffic in a car lane.

Mushroom or not, biking has soared in the last five years as an adult recreational activity, both at home and abroad, and the accessories for this leisure sport have become increasingly elaborate.

"Next year," the husband said, "I'm going to get one of those nifty little rear-view mirrors to attach to my helmet."

Turned out that the most vital acquisition for this trip into an Eastern Bloc country wasn't a helmet. It was a visa. Hungary is one of the most free-spirited of the Communist countries in Eastern Europe, we were told. We'd be allowed to bicycle anywhere we wanted. That was true. But getting *into* the country was a bit of a production. Our biking tour group had to meet Austria/Hungary border officials at a precise time on the afternoon of our entry so that we could all cross over together. Getting bikers in a foreign country to meet anywhere at a precise time is not easy, but somehow we accomplished it.

Waiting for us on the other side of the border was the manager of the hotel where we were to stay for two nights, the Szechenyi Castle. His name was Peter Jakab, 27, and he accompanied us on his own bike all the way to our government-owned accommodation. Although private investments are allowed in Hungary, this castle hotel was publically subsidized, as are all hotels of 10 rooms or more.

Peter turned out to be a charming young entrepreneur, who told us he is a member of the country's democratic party. He softened the feeling of a chilly Communist welcome considerably by having his white-jacketed hotel waiters greet us with glasses of "booster" cocktails, a typical Hungarian drink containing two kinds of brandy schnapps mixed with white wine and a fresh cherry at the bottom.

After biking 58-kilometers (36-miles) that day, during which we were punished by strong headwinds, the potent cocktails were a welcome "boost" indeed, and left most of us weaving straight to our rooms, where we fell on our duvet-covered beds and slept until dinner.

That evening, the waiters were so amazed by our new French bikes that they asked if they could try them out. They also wanted to see under the hood of our bike van and eventually took it for a spin as well. For all the new-found economic freedom in Hungary, they obviously don't have as many shiny new vehicles as you find in the neighboring countries to the west.

What the Hungarians do have, and what droves of the neighboring Austrians cross the border in pursuit of, is good food at cheap prices. (One warning: When you change your Austrian shillings into Hungarian florins, you may be stuck with them unless you spend all the money. The government allows you to change only half of it back into another country's currency.)

Our favorite dishes during our stay in Hungary were the pancakes in paprika cream sauce, the caviar omelets, the stuffed cabbage (we felt like stuffed cabbages ourselves much of the time we were there), chocolate dessert pancakes filled with hazelnut stuffing and covered with warm chocolate sauce, and the moist cherry strudel served at the end of an outdoor picnic on the grounds of the Esterhazy summer palace in the town of Fertod.

Luckily for us, we didn't have to order these things from a menu. Hungarian is a wildly exotic language to our eyes and ears, and we couldn't even decipher the words for "soup" or "dessert" on the menus, much less navigate the variations on unheard-of main courses. Thank goodness for a tour guide who can speak the language when you need one.

When it comes to music, fortunately, no language skills are required. At least on a menu. Both Austria and Hungary are rich in the history of music, and the music is what we remember most about our bike trip here. Even more than the beer.

Franz Joseph Haydn spent his summers conducting and composing in the 18th-century, and as we passed by the concert hall where he worked, we heard the sweet sounds of Schumann being played live on a beautiful grand piano. The pianist turned out to be a British woman from London, member of an amateur chamber music tour group, testing the acoustics. Putting our bikes aside we sneaked inside the hall and, for a glorious hour sitting in the back row, we were transported by the music.

The most thrilling musical experience we had was just over the Austria border in Eisenstadt, where our biking route eventually took us. Its many-windowed, gilt-and-blue concert hall boasts the second-best acoustics in Austria (the first being the opera house at Vienna). Here, Haydn worked for 30 years, living in a house just around the corner from the palace.

Although we were not able to attend a live concert there, the palace tour included a CD rendition of Haydn's Symphony No. 85 in B-flat major ("The Queen"). Listening, we felt like royalty.

Earlier, we had biked through the tiny town of Raiding, Austria, home of Franz Liszt. In nearby Herzogenburg, at a stunningly ornate church rebuilt by two of the greatest architects of the Austrian Baroque, we happened upon the preparations for a wedding. Enthralled, we listened to the organist practicing Bach's D minor Toccata and Fugue on the grand Baroque organ in the choir loft.

Later, in the gorgeous, onion-domed 12th-century Heiligenkreuz Monastery, with inlaid wooden cabinets that took two monks 30 years to complete, we were treated to a noontime Gregorian chant by the 55 Cistercian monks who still live in the half-Romanesque, half-Gothic church.

And we heard much more pedestrian contemporary music throughout the trip, including the polkas of the beer hall musicians with their accordions and fiddles, and the soulful music of the gypsies who serenaded us at the picnic in Fertod.

Tour guides are there when you need them.

If France is the eating-and-drinking trip and northern Italy is the wildflower-and-wine trip, the Hapsburg Empire is the music-and-church bells trip. The sound of music is everywhere. Indoors in the churches and the concert halls.

Outdoors, where you hear the *dong... dong... dong... dong* of the deep-throated church bells echoing over the countryside, and the constant cheeping and warbling of the birds that sing from dawn to dusk in the bushes along the lanes.

Of course, this area has its share of flowers, too. On our previous trips we've seen many fields scattered with wild poppies, but it was in Hungary that we saw them growing as actual crops, the white, purple and red blossoms stretching to the horizon like a floral ocean. They're used in Hungary for all manner of sweets, even poppyseed ice cream. Roses, too, were blooming in great profusion. One of our hotel balconies overlooked a "rosarium," where thousands of them gave off a fragrance that drifted up and into our room.

Perhaps it was the new bikes we were riding, but on this trip our stamina seemed to have noticeably improved, as had our conditioning. The softly rolling hills - which the troops of old Franz Josef I, the Hapsburg emperor from 1848 to 1916, marched up and down during the losing battles of his waning empire – scarcely strained our uphill muscles.

But by the end of the sixth day, when we wheeled into Baden, Austria after an unusually long ride – 40-plus miles - the city's hot sulfur baths were most inviting.

Baden's mineral baths are famous for curing whatever ails you, and what ailed us on this day was every last one of our "scarcely strained" biking muscles, which were crying out for respite from the road.

We waded into the municipal pools and took our places among a throng of hefty Austrian men and women wearing an array of skimpy swimsuits. The baths left our tired bodies cleansed and reinvigorated but with a peculiar odor that hovered around us at the dinner table that evening. Everyone tried to ignore it.

The trip was drawing to a close. The next morning our tour group awoke to rainy grey conditions and we discovered that all the seats were wet when we went to fetch the bikes. It was disappointing weather to end on, but according to the local custom it may have been our own fault. Austrians say that when it rains, it means someone didn't finish their soup. We all wondered who was the culprit.

It wasn't really a problem, however. Pedaling in the rain is not ideal on these "luxury" bike tours, but it comes with the territory – luxury or not. And for most of the people who take these outdoor trips, a little bad weather is scarcely enough to dampen the spirit.

At the farewell dinner that evening, after hot baths and a longer than usual wine tasting session, the mood was as sunny as ever, filled with toasts and jokes and silly anecdotes about the trip. One of the offerings was a poem we wrote concerning all the nights on the trip that had been spent in combat with our

Austrian duvets (doo-VAYs), the traditional puffy cover that serves as sheet, blanket, comforter, spread and sham in that country. The wife read it out loud to many hoots and hollers of agreement:

When you sleep the Hapsburg way,
It's almost always with duvet,
Mass of covers, tucked away.

Puffed and starched, our white duvet
On the bed it calmly lay -
But under it, we joined the fray
Of those who seek to find the way
To stay just halfway covered
By duvet.

Give us a good old blanket, pray;
Curse the ornery, perverse duvet!
Chilly legs can't seem to stay
Completely 'neath this damn duvet.

Half the body, Austrians say,
At least stays warm
Beneath duvets.

Half the body – we tourists say –
Gets hot as hell beneath duvet.
The other half is cold as ice.
Damn, the covers stray... just fall away.
It never fails with these duvets.

Sleeping alone is bad enough
When you're buried alive under one of these puffs.
But a husband and wife under a single duvet?
"Forget it" she declares. "It's too hot to play."
Lord, when they finally lay us away
Let them box us in pine, bury us in clay,
Burn our remains and throw them away.

Just please, dear Lord, we fervently pray:
Don't put us under
An Austrian duvet!

The trip was over. After the farewell festivities that night, we climbed the steep winding stairs of our 18th Century hotel and unlocked the door to our room. There sat our huge, ornate, antique wooden bed. And on it lay the biggest, puffiest, heaviest white duvet in all of Hungary. Without another word we threw off our clothes and slipped beneath it.

That night we slept the sleep of the dead. We weren't too hot and we weren't too cold – or if we were, we didn't notice it.

We didn't play, either. Maybe it was the off-setting odor of the sulfur baths that still clung to our bodies. Or maybe it was because we were just too darned tired. The hills of Hungary had finally taken their toll. We slept in peace.

The authors take a flower break.

LA RIOJA, SPAIN

Spanish villages are often an uphill challenge.

La Rioja

December, 1990

"The grain was just beginning to ripen and the fields were full of poppies. The pastureland was green, and there were fine trees, and sometimes big rivers and chateaux off in the trees."

"In back of the plateau were the mountains, and every way you looked there were other mountains, and ahead the road stretched out white across the plain going toward Pamplona."

-Excepts from "The Sun Also Rises" by Ernest Hemingway

It is very easy to feel like a character in one of Ernest Hemingway's novels when you retrace the path that the bulls take through the streets of this city each summer in the annual ritual of machismo that Hemingway's novels made famous.

To anyone familiar with Hemingway's writing, his presence is powerful throughout Spain and particularly in Pamplona, where the writer's handsome face, cast in bronze, stares out over the "Paseo de Hemingway," directly in front of the municipal bullring.

But we had not come to race bulls. We were here to ride bicycles - this time through the northern Spanish provinces of Navarre and La Rioja...

The second day we biked into the hills with the two artists, Sumner and Helen. A breeze was at our backs, funneling off the slopes of the Sierra de Cantabria far in the distance, and the sun was in our eyes as we pedaled up the black macadam road. Two vultures circled in the brazen blue sky above the fields of dry dirt, and it was good to be alive, the kind of day that tastes sweet in your mouth like a bottle of white wine kept cool in the waters of the Ebro.

This was our fifth bicycle trip to Europe, our first in the fall, in what has become a love affair with this mode of travel. Our previous trips have been to Bordeaux, northern Italy, Provence and, last year, to Austria and Hungary.

As always, our tour company provided the 18-speed bikes, the van to carry our luggage, the accommodations in a variety of exotic chateaus, castles and abbeys, and the special meals featuring the food of the region. We provide the pedal power.

On paper, the plan for this trip was the same as the others. But the Spanish countryside in autumn is altogether different than France in springtime.

Spain in autumn is brown and dry and starkly beautiful, a land in repose, a harsh and stubborn terrain of empty fields and wondrous silence.

Biking through the province of Navarre in northern Spain in autumn is a solitary, almost mystical experience, passing across a lunar surface of faraway mountains and terraced valleys, intersected by long narrow roads almost totally devoid of people and cars.

One day, biking from Olite to San Adrian, almost two hours went by before a car passed us on the road. A cyclist can look out on a vista stretching for miles and miles, as we did biking to the little Basque town of Ujue, and see no sign of civilization except occasional flocks of sheep that range across the arid land. No billboards, no restaurants, no farmers, no fences.

Like America's frontier in the 1800s, fences are almost unheard of in this part of Spain. The sheep and goats wander through the countryside tended by wizened shepherds and mongrel dogs that chase after the strays, jumping on their backs and keeping the animals in line with the discipline of a traffic cop.

Occasionally, one also comes across herds of black bulls being bred for the *corrida* - the bull ring - as we did in a ravine outside of Miranda.

The sun rose red over Calahorra on the fourth day; there would be rain on the way to Logrono. We had churros for breakfast - fried dough, dipped in cups of thick hot chocolate - and left at 9 o'clock, wheeling down the long, straight road that runs from the town bluff to the valley below.

In the middle of the morning the rain came down from the mountains, a soft mist that formed little beads of water on our Gore-Tex biking suits. We found an abandoned shepherd's shack in the middle of a field, empty except for a pair of old slippers on the dirt floor. The rain had stopped when we left and we raced past fields of green asparagus and wild fennel, quickening the pace to get to the tour picnic by noon. We found it at an old Roman aqueduct outside the town of Lodosa; two young tour guides had already laid out the food on a table under one of the stone arches.

We broke loaves of fresh Spanish bread into pieces and poured olive oil over them and ate the bread with manchezo cheese from La Mancha and blue cabrales cheese and goat cheese and garbanza (chick peas with Bermuda onions soaked in vinaigrette) and slices of Spanish sausage known as chorizo, and fat green Spanish olives and potato tortilla and red peppers marinated in olive oil and garlic, and salad with white asparagus, a Spanish delicacy.

We drank bottles of dark Rioja red, and crisp Rioja white wine, and then we ate almond cookies and hunks of dark chocolate with glasses of apple schnapps, and then we climbed back on our bikes and pedaled up the dirt road paralleling the aqueduct and turned left on the road to Logrono. A patch of blue sky was showing to the north and we could see the spiky ridges of the Pyrenees in the distance and we knew the next day would be warm and fine, and that it would be good to be biking in Spain.

One of the particular pleasures of these bike tours of Europe is the food of

Farmhouse for sale — cheap — in Rioja.

each country. This was especially true of Spain, where the variety of the cuisine and the novelty in which it was served were surprising.

Traveling through a country in the fall instead of the spring has the advantage of the season's harvest, and, as we moved from the barren plains of the Navarre to the greener vineyard country of the Rioja, we knew the vegetables and fruits on our plates at night were only hours away from the field.

If you go to northern Spain - on or off a bicycle - be sure not to miss a meal that begins with a plate of *migas*, a mixture of crumbled bread and ham cooked in oil and garlic over a charcoal brazier in the middle of your table... or a plate of succulent baby lamb chops grilled on an indoor hearth over grapevine twig embers that crackle and hiss in a dim room... or, *mio Dio!* a dessert of *cuajada*, a curdled yogurt-junket mixture served in a ceramic pot with a pitcher of warm honey and sugar-glazed walnuts.

In Logrono, we were introduced to an entirely new way of taking dinner: standing up. Walking through a four-block labyrinth of tiny bistros, always standing at the bar, we grazed on tapas, the bite-sized portions of food (served with shot-sized glasses of wine) that are a way of life in Spain. We tasted cold squid salad in one place; warm mushroom sandwiches in another; tiny steamed shrimp in a third; and puffs of baked cheese in a closet-sized cafe next door. Tapas are so specialized in this town that there are different places for serving flat and round mushrooms.

Even when middle-aged bikers haven't overindulged in Spanish cuisine, their clothes are not especially flattering. The apparel is made of skintight material in garish colors, often with the name of the manufacturer written all over the front and down the sides, making the cyclist look like some sort of foreign road sign. On men, it's worse, because the pants end at the knees, leaving hairy bare legs bare beneath all the color. Worse still, the protective plastic-foam helmets give these weekend warriors the appearance of alien space invaders.

It was quite a surprise, therefore, to be asked by the locals in northern Spain if we were pilgrims.

As it turned out, our biking route was the same one penitents have used for centuries, traveling from France to Galicia on the west coast of Spain over the Camino de Santiago de Compostela. While the earlier voyagers always trekked by foot (some in chains as a sign of their contrition), their modern equivalents frequently make the journey by bicycle, hence the confusion about us, surprising as it was.

Spain is rich with religious history and legend, and if you doubt it, be sure to visit the church of Santo Domingo de la Calzoda in LaGuardia. It has

Spain in autumn - a starkly beautiful land in repose.

something no other church in the world has: a live rooster and hen living in an elaborate cage in the sanctuary.

Legend has it that, around 1350, a cooked chicken and rooster came back to life at the exact moment a hanged pilgrim enjoyed the same reprieve - and ever since, a white rooster and hen have been kept on display in the opulent church in honor of that miraculous event.

Early invasions by the Moors left the craggy hills of the region dotted with spectacular old castles that make great photo opportunities.

And if you really, really want to go back in time, be sure not to miss the ruins uncovered at La Hoya dating back to 1300 BC, the oldest in Spain.

A farmer was hunting quail up in the hills. You could hear the 'humph-humph-humph' of his shotgun as we biked out of Haro on the last day of the trip and headed down the empty road toward Anguciana. The early light was cool and clean, like the shallow waters of the Rio Tiron, which we crossed an hour later.

Black-and-white magpies flashed across the road ahead and we rode in silence, heads down, muscles moving in rhythm, a sensual pressure of feet on pedal, the blur of pavement flowing beneath the wheels.

The road crossed through a series of vineyards, the small tough vines that flourish in the soil of Rioja heavy with grapes, blue-black against the dark green leaves. We passed through the sun-splashed pueblos of Chihuri and Castanares and, in Banares, a woman sold us some sweet red wine, pouring it directly from a giant keg into two empty glass bottles that barely fit in our bike bags, and we drank the wine with bread and goat cheese later in the afternoon, sitting on a hillside in the sun. We stayed there until the light grew thin and the air turned chill and then we biked back into the town for the last night of the trip, and after dinner ordered a bottle of tempranillo that we drank in our room.

NORTHERN CALIFORNIA

California's wineries always welcome bikers.

Wine Country

August, 1993

Question: What country has more vineyards than France, more flowers than Austria, better wine than Italy, better food than Hungary – and fewer tourists than Spain?

Answer: The wine country of northern California.

We can attest to it. We've bicycled through all of the above.

With the exchange rate in Europe making the American dollar a poor cousin to the franc, we decided this spring -- after eight years of cycling through the vineyards of southern France, northern Italy, eastern Austria, western Hungary and northern Spain -- that this was the year to "go American." We signed up for a bike trip through five of the most famous valleys of the California wine country: Alexander, Dry Creek, Napa, Sonoma and Russian River.

So how does an American bike trip measure up to all those European experiences? We would not characterize what follows as a scientific survey, but here, for bikers and oenophiles alike, are some of our findings:

• Hardly anyone in California speaks an exotic foreign language. This has pluses and minuses. On the one hand, it's easier to ask directions and order wine. On the other hand, you can't impress your spouse by speaking a language you took in high school (ok, making a fool of yourself in front of the locals in the process). And in California, the beautiful French phrase "cabernet sauvignon" is shortened to the more utilitarian, but inelegant, "cab."

• The roads are better in America, with generous bike paths at the side of the road; but the drivers in Europe are more courteous. They hardly ever honk and absolutely never give you the bird as they pass.

• There are very few ancient and picturesque castles and chateaux in America. About as ancient as a Californian lodging gets is the Victoriana decor of the 1881 mansion Madrona Manor, our first night's stay. Europe may have its antique claw-footed bathtubs but has very few high-tech bathrooms. You've not experienced physical delight until you've jumped into the muscle-pulsing

Grapevines and bikers cope with steep hills in California.

Jacuzzi of the Vintage Inn in Yountville after biking through Dry Creek and Alexander Valleys on a warm spring day.

• The roses in France and Italy are lovely and red and planted randomly at the ends of grapevine rows and along the road to lure insects away from the vines. But they're puny compared to the ones you see in Sonoma. The roses in northern California are the size of grapefruits and, in addition to being planted in the vineyards, they are arranged in ordered, massive formal gardens in all colors. Many vineyard visits in California include garden tours.

• As for wildflowers, both parts of the world have their share, but what's considered "wild" in one might be found as a dinner table centerpiece in another. In Europe, farmers mow the red poppies because they're considered weeds, while in northern California, the majestic calla lily – carried by many a bride down the aisle -- grows wild.

• The thermal winds that come up daily over Bodega Bay and sweep across the California coastal vineyards are just as obnoxious to bikers as the mistral in France, the seasonal wind that comes up every afternoon in Provence. Both seem to be coming directly at you wherever your turn, and both seemingly want to knock you off your seat. Never before, as on the way to Bodega Bay, have we experienced the feeling of pedaling straight uphill while going downhill because of that dratted headwind.

• People who bike in Europe come in all sizes, shapes and ages, and dress in blacks and grays and skirts and babushkas and sensible brown shoes, while most of those who bike in California look 23 with thighs of steel; they obviously live on the Stairmaster when not at work or asleep. They wear neon reds and blues and whites with wacky, loud cartoons and stripes, and their helmets are shiny and tapered. On our trip they were not content with the 33-mile average daily ride; this, for them, was primarily a vacation they could take without having to miss their daily spin classes. At the cocktail hour, many eschewed the wine, clearly worried that it might impede their ability to pedal efficiently the next morning. When the next morning came, they always started off before the rest of us and we never saw them on the road the rest of the day. This was because they always chose to ride the most excruciatingly difficult route listed for each

California biking trails often present ocean views.

day's ride – the longest routes possible, the ones that took them over the steepest hills, circling up and around our piddling shortest-route-possible roads from one town to the next. Around mid-afternoon, pedaling with the same bullet speed you see on the Tour de France, they shot through a final intersection, tires smoking, and braked to a stop in front of our next hotel. By the time we dragged in late each afternoon, tired and sweaty, they were already bathed, changed and waiting for dinner.

• When it comes to wine, the French think they rule the world. But (sorry, Pierre) California has caught up. Fact is, there are more wineries in Sonoma Valley alone than in all of France. Or maybe it was just our imagination after all the wine tastings we had before 11 a.m. on this trip. You begin to lose count. More than 100 of California's most noted wineries and champagneries were within a radius of 35 kilometers of the Madrona Manor.

European wineries, by the way, are ancient, yellow stucco buildings that are serviceable and perfectly nice, but there is little variety in their architectural style. Expecting the same utilitarian buildings in California, we were astonished to find that American vineyard owners, blessed with witty imaginations and plenty of the cash necessary to own a winery here, often decorate their vineyards with delightful design surprises. The ultramodern, classically columned Clos Pegase winery, designed by Michael Graves, houses a valuable art collection that includes a wonderful five-foot-high brass thumb sticking up out of one of the rows of grapevines, as if some artistic Gulliver were testing the row for perspective. The Monticello winery features a miniature copy of Thomas Jefferson's home in Virginia, complete with red bricks and white picket fences.

But the most amazing winery we saw was the 1 1/2-year-old Codorniu, designed by Barcelona architect Domingo Triay and carved into the side of a grassy hill in Napa Valley so that only its fountains and windows are above ground. Cordorniu incorporates the "berm" system that uses earth to help insulate the wines from the northern California sun. As you bike up the winding driveway, the structure reveals itself as a sort of Mayan temple, and from the terrace, sipping the popular sparkling wine that merges pear, fresh cream and toasted nut flavors in one glass, it feels as though you can see all the way to the Yucatan peninsula.

What about food?

The cuisine in Europe is the exquisite result of a long historical tradition of using the freshest products for traditional regional recipes. The cuisine in northern California, on the other hand, is a brash, young experimental array of dishes that taste fresher and healthier than anything we ate in Europe. Baby greens are so varied that a salad can include thirteen different varieties. These are a daily offering in the California wine country. Crusty sourdough or walnut bread is as good as any baguette. Bowls of perfect strawberries and cantaloupe reminded us of where all that fruit comes from during our own East Coast winters.

The best tastes of California food and wine came, for us, after a five-hour bike ride to a late lunch on the patio of Domaine Chandon, a champagnery set into its own manicured park in the charming town of Yountville. It began with a kir royale and mimosa using the house's own champagne and continued with perfectly roasted rabbit and garlics with artichoke ragout, squab in its delicate reduced sauce with fresh peas and puree of squash, and for dessert a warm chocolate feuillette (a boxlike pastry) filled with fresh strawberry ice cream, topped with chocolate sauce. Domaine Chandon Restaurant has a four-star rating, an honor bestowed on fewer than 300 of 32,000 restaurants across the country. After lunching there, we understood why it had been granted that distinction.

Emerging from a redwood forest.

At the end of a European biking day, the options include crashing on your bed, still in biking clothes, or chatting up a group of interesting people from everywhere in the world at the bar. In northern California the choices are funkier. They include settling your sore body into a tub of steaming mud at the famed Calistoga baths, or a soothing massage at the Sonoma Mission Inn and Spa. We might have missed these special pleasures, incidentally, if our tour company, Backroads, hadn't steered us in their direction. That's one of the advantages of signing up with a tour group rather than going alone -- making your own reservations and carrying your belongings with you to save money.

There are others. You've heard of road rage? Well, road *rhapsody* is when one of the friendly guides in those ubiquitous little Backroads vans comes along at the right moment to change a flat bike tire for you, or serves a luxurious picnic lunch for the group in a shaded grove beside the road, or pulls up next to you on a hill and hands you a bag of energy snacks. Or, most definitely, finding your luggage mysteriously waiting for you in your room when you arrive at that night's lodging after a long day on the road.

Bottom line:

Nothing takes the place of ancient stone castles and quaint little European villages with cobblestone streets and window boxes -- but the mystic serenity of redwood forests, the tropical palms along the rocky Pacific Ocean coastline, the giant purple flowers bordering the edge of the road, and the wide open expanses of hilly California pastureland come close.

You will never forget the sweet fragrances of freshly cut hay at midday as you bike the roads of Italy, or the musty smells of fermenting grapes in the oaken casks of a French wine cellar. But you will never get the spicy tang of eucalyptus trees and the sweet heavy aroma of orange blossoms out of your mind, either, after cycling in northern California.

With the sun on your face and two pencil-thin touring wheels beneath, an open road with unknown adventure ahead and a hillside picnic including the region's best wines in the offing, it really doesn't seem to matter much which coast, or which country, you're biking.

BURGUNDY, FRANCE

Pedaling through a silent vineyard in Burgundy.

Burgundy

August, 1995

Where else in civilized Europe but here in Burgundy does a man encourage you to spit on the floor of his own home?

Our host made it seem like the most natural thing in the world.

We were standing in the cool, cavernous wine cellar of the Chateau Genot-Boulanger, and the owner was presiding at our first wine tasting on the first day of our bike trip through this wine-obsessed region. It was 10:45 a.m.... a perfect time to start tasting vintage Burgundy reds and whites.

"Please feel free to expectorate the remains of your wine onto our gravel floor," he said, as he did so himself. "It adds to the humidity, and that's good for the wooden barrels and the corks, which is good for the wine."

In Burgundy, where the vine and the grape (particularly the great pinot noir) reign supreme, whatever is good for the wine is good for life itself. Virtually everyone in this French province is devoted to enhancing it, nurturing it, aging it, protecting it, discussing it and, ultimately, drinking it. And so, as tasty as this wine was, we dutifully spat it out on his floor to make room on our tongues for more.

This was our third bike trip to France (our sixth to Europe overall). We had thought Bordeaux was the ultimate wine country. But Burgundy makes Bordeaux look like Davenport, Iowa -- oenologically speaking, that is. The karma of winemaking is all around you.

You feel it in the vineyards, which stretch for miles in all directions.

You feel it walking the ancient cobblestone streets of Beaune, under which are two levels of wine cellars that date back to the first century AD. (Established by monks who first planted grape vines in this region, the so-called "caves" are

From narrow vineyard lanes to narrow village streets.

under the town's large church as well. The great wines rest beneath the altar itself.)

You feel the wine karma in shop windows. (They are filled with wine accouterments of every size and description, from ancient corkscrews to beautiful little "tastevins," the shallow silver taster's cups with raised indentations to reflect the color of the wine and exhibit its clarity.)

You sense its presence in the food you eat. (The salad dressings in the restaurants are usually served with very little vinegar so as not to ruin the tongue for wine; the delicious eggs called "oeufs en murette" that are served as a first course or on top of a salad, slightly red in color, are poached in -- you guessed it -- red wine.)

Even our first hotel's name reflected this magnificent obsession with wine. It was called Le Cep, as in "the stem of the vine."

Everyone knows that great wine should accompany great cuisine, and Burgundian cuisine, we discovered, represents the Olympics of eating. The late A.J. Liebling, an epicure who knew a lot about both, wrote that Burgundian food is "peasant cooking elevated to its greatest possible heights." He also observed that "you need a solid stomach to live on Burgundian cooking, but Burgundian cooking develops solid stomachs."

We can second that. Our stomachs were a bit flabby at the start of the trip, but they were rock solid by the end after all the Burgundian food we ate. Our gastric juices and ruminant muscles were working round the clock. And ours weren't the only ones. Our biking group consisted of 20 stomachs. Some were Canadian, some were American, two were Australian. But they were all wimpy, it seemed. At various times during the week, one or another of them fell victim to an early morning flu-like weakness, brought on not by a virus so much as the terrines and pates, the escargots and mushrooms, the chevres, the beef bourgninon, the creme brulee and the other killer desserts – three in succession at one of our meals. The discomfort came not from salmonella but from excess. Gout hung in the air.

Our very first lunch was advertised as a "picnic," taken at a rustic little roadside place called "Au Plaisir du Ventre," which, loosely translated, means "Everything Your Gut Wishes." After we finished, the only thing our guts wished for was a chance to lie down by the side of the road and digest.

The picnic consisted of whole roasted chickens, three different pates, three heavily-dressed salads, white asparagus, cheeses – both hard and soft -- wines, breads, white bean tarts, pizzas, and a strawberry cream cake that the chef, who was the French version of Luciano Pavarotti from the neck down, whipped up that morning.

That was the start of a gastronomical marathon that continued for the rest of the trip. Six days and six pounds later, we staggered to our final dinner at a starred Michelin restaurant near our chateau in Chambertin-Musigny.

More on the food later. There was lots of it, take our word for it. But in Burgundy – *quelle surpris!* – it's the wines, not the food, that are the real show stoppers. And we had a lot of them, too. Accompanying our farewell meal were limitless bottles of Bourgogne Blanc Chardonnay, Chambolle-Musigny Premier Cru, and Chambertin "Clos de Beze" Grand Cru. These were local wines, but not just any local wines. They happen to be among the best in the world.

No wonder the old dukes of Burgundy, including Charles the Reckless and Philip the Bold, fought to the end to keep their region completely separate from the rest of France. They knew they owned the mother lode of precious wines, and from earliest times these vineyards have been passed down from generation to generation.

Burgundy cuisine is almost as important as the wine.

With family division and more and more offspring claiming their share, one man's vineyard today can be as small as a tenth of an acre. Even that postage stamp-sized piece of land, though, would be worth about $50,000 if anyone were willing to sell it.

Since the vineyards in Burgundy are smaller than those in Bordeaux, this region produces much less wine than the latter, and most of it stays in France. The annual production simply runs out before most of it can get to the U.S. or anywhere else. That makes Burgundian wine more precious than Bordeaux wines, both to the pocketbook and to the palate of those in the know.

One of our fellow bikers, a knowledgeable wine aficionado who chose this trip specifically because of the wine, got off his bicycle and fell to his knees when he reached the Romanee-Conti vineyards. At first we thought he had had an accident, but no, he had dropped to the ground on purpose, getting down to smell and feel this dirt with his own nose and fingers, paying personal homage to the famous soil that produces such nectar.

Tour guides are always fluent in the language and customs of the host country, but ours was a bona fide oenologist as well, having just completed a two-year master's program at the nearby University of Dijon.

His name was Ted Talley, and he spoke in rhapsodic phrases about both the wines of the region and the grapes they came from, not to mention the enchanted soil.

Standing beside a vineyard in the Cote d'Or, he noted that the Romanee-Conti vintage was "a lady's wine -- lacy and delicate." A little farther down the road we came to the vines of the Chambertin. According to Talley, these produced the previous wine's "masculine counterpart." This is a "beefed-up red like a man on steroids," he declared. "It's robust, weighty and powerful." Warming to his description of this famous Burgundy, he added: "It doesn't stop and it doesn't drop. It doesn't just leave you there. It goes around the corner."

Wine, of course, isn't the only famous fermentation of Burgundy. The black currants grown in this region make the best cassis in the world, according to those in the know. At the Domaine Lucien Jacob in the tiny hilltop town of Echevronne, we tasted this dark red liqueur in three flavors: regular currant (the only one legitimately called "cassis"), blackberry and raspberry. Combined with a white burgundy, any of the three make the delicious cocktail kir – or, when mixed with a sparkling white burgundy, a "Kir Royale." We had one of each before pedaling down into the town of Nuits-St-Georges for lunch at an outdoor cafe.

Earlier that morning, biking out of the town of Serrigny following an early morning rain shower, we had passed fields heavy with the scent of fresh manure mixed with the sweet fragrance of lavender, roses and hay. Earth aromas like these are a memorable part of biking in Europe, a special pleasure, never to be enjoyed in the interior of an air-conditioned tour bus. And in Burgundy, the earth itself is a large part of what makes the region special, since the best of Burgundy all seems to be *sous bois*, or underground -- from the mushrooms, to the roots of the vineyards, to the wines in the cellars under the streets, to the snails that come to the table in fine French restaurants as l'escargots.

…Which brings us back to that over-the-top menu at our farewell dinner. The one we mentioned above.

It began with a heavy appetizer that was, yes, *sous bois*: a mushroom cream soup both delicious and rich, a sufficient dinner all by itself. After the last elegant spoonful we steadied ourselves for our main course. Wishful thinking, it turned out. The second appetizer arrived minutes later -- succulent escargots carefully arranged on the plate with generous pieces of cooked lobster and slender slices of *pommes gratinee*. Exquisitely rich. We assumed it would take the place of the fish course. But no. When the next course arrived and the silver covers were triumphantly lifted (each new arrival was dramatically introduced with a simultaneous raising of the gleaming covers by the many waiters), not one but three kinds of fish were revealed, each in its own sauce.

By now our eyes were beginning to glaze over. We stared nervously at the three additional forks at each setting. Could they possibly augur three more courses to come? The answer was delivered moments later when the waiters and waitresses trooped in carrying the "main" course. It turned out to be tender slices of roast duckling in a fragrant wine sauce, a $45 plate by itself in any New York restaurant. By then we were teetering on the edge of digestive shock.

Finally, the dessert. In came a large silver tray of lacy cookies, chocolate truffles, *petits fours* and cream-covered fruit, a presentation so beautiful that many grabbed their cameras to photograph it before devouring all the goodies, an exquisite ending to a meal fit for kings.

But, alas, it wasn't the end. It was apparently just something to keep us occupied while the waiters brought in the real dessert: eggshells with their tops cut off to reveal a vanilla mousse, decorated with chocolate-tipped rolled cookie sticks. We finished that and set down our napkins, grateful to have survived.

But our relief was premature. Groaning, we suddenly realized that the "real" dessert was about to be served. It consisted of a large cylinder of strawberry and cream gelatinous mousse, encircled by a thin chocolate/vanilla cake roll on a plate decorated with two flavors of sorbet and several pretty slices of fresh fruit.

Mercifully, with one last bite of vanilla cake role, the farewell dinner came to an end. The only thing that stood between us and our beds was a glass of sweet botrytised Chardonnay, served on a silver tray by a waitress who looked to be in her eighties. She brought back the memory of a woman who had presided at one of our wine tastings along our route. Her name was Madam Masson, a staunch monarchist who railed against the French Revolution as she trudged us up and down the stone steps of her fortified home, ordering us into cotton slippers before we stepped onto the shiny wood floor of her ancient living room. From there she led us down to her private wine cellar, where the visit almost ended disastrously. Standing amid the oaken casks in her cave, a member of our group took a flash photograph of Madame Masson as she was pouring the wine with an 80-year-old hand that was steadier than any of ours.

"Stop! No flashbulbs!" the old woman screamed.

Sheepishly, our companion quickly put his camera away, assuming Madame Masson was vain and didn't want her picture taken. That wasn't the problem, however. Madame Masson wasn't thinking about Madame Masson. Something else.

"The bright light disturbs the wine!" explained the grande old dame of Burgundy -- possibly the only place in the world where wine is treated like fine art.

CORSICA & SARDINIA

Hairpin turns and stunning views in Corsica.

Corsica & Sardinia

March, 1997

Question: How can you travel in France and Italy without ever setting foot on the mainland of Europe?

Answer: Take a vacation to the islands of Corsica and Sardinia. They're Europe but they're not. That's where we took our latest bike trip. We biked, we hiked, we rode in a restored turn-of-the-century steam-powered train around these two European outposts. And, in the end, we traveled from one to the other in a high-speed cigarette boat. (Corsica is a part of France and Sardinia is Italian).

Not every member of our gung-ho group of biking enthusiasts took the boat ride, however. One of them made the 12-mile trip from Corsica to Sardinia in the water. She swam.

Whatever way you go -- by plane, boat, or Australian crawl – put Corsica and Sardinia high on your list when it comes to European biking destinations. If you like beautiful beaches, rugged mountain vistas, quaint old villages, friendly people, quiet back roads and lots of good food and wine, you'll love both of these two islands. And if you can speak French and/or Italian, you've got it made.

Our bike tour company had never gone to either Corsica or Sardinia. The tour leaders didn't really know what to expect, and neither did we.

The daily ground rules were the same as for all luxury bike tours: mount your multi-gear bike each morning; try to follow the hand-drawn map the guide gives you; make the pedals go around until you reach that night's accommodation. Your luggage will beat you there in a van.

From Ajaccio on the southeast coast of Corsica, where Napoleon was born, we had our first look at the island's breathtaking seascapes, blue-green coves and miles of craggy mountains in the distance, which evoked nervous worries about whether our calf muscles could take us up and over those behemoths.

Not to worry. The route would follow the foothills along the coasts of both Corsica and Sardinia, avoiding the steepest terrain. It was challenging in some stretches but not impossible, and the views were so spectacular along the coastlines that pushing uphill for a morning or an afternoon was more than worth the effort. The downhill glides, of course, were pure joy.

Corsica, called the Isle of Beauty, is surprisingly unpopulated. In ancient times, the coastline was invaded by so many other countries that the Corsicans moved into the mountainous interior to hide in the dense foliage known as the "maquis." The island at that time had a serious mosquito problem, with death from malaria a real threat to anyone who lived along the warm coastlines.

With the interior of the country considered the most valuable, Corsican men inherited the inland property while their sisters inherited the cheaper land along the ocean. Guess who now holds the most valuable real estate on Corsica?

When it comes to waterfront commercial development, Corsica has preserved its beaches for the future – unintentionally.

Any foreign company trying to build a high-rise hotel on the coast of the island is frequently in for an unpleasant surprise. That's because the FLNC, or Front Liberation National Corse -- the nationalists who want to split from France -- have a nasty habit of visiting such sites in the middle of the night and bombing the foundations to smithereens before the structures are completed. The result is an unspoiled natural coastline, one that made the real estate moguls on our bike trip drool as they bicycled along the ridges of uninhabited, undeveloped oceanfront land overlooking the turquoise waters of the Mediterranean. The gorgeous white sand beaches were largely empty on the beautiful days in May when we were there.

Oh, there's an occasional beachgoer -- nude, of course. That's the Corsican way. There might be a tiny, family-owned restaurant on a cliff with a view of the water every so often, but for long stretches, the land is free of human activity.

That's even truer as you go toward the interior. For bicyclists, an empty road is a perfect road, and in Corsica most of them are perfect for most of the time. The back roads of this 3,350-square-mile island make the lonely bike paths of Burgundy feel crowded. You don't see a car from one hour to the next.

Granted, part of this peace and quiet resulted from the fact that we were there ahead of the tourist influx. But even in the high season, the number of ferry boats to the island is tightly controlled so as to limit the number of visitors, and berths on the ferries are so precious that one must book them two years in advance. (Only 250,000 Corsicans live on the island year round.)

If the emptiness of Corsica is remarkable, so is its cleanliness.

The sight of a piece of wrapping paper at the side of the road was cause for great surprise. Only occasionally did we see any trash barrels, carefully enclosed in wire trash bins, and we never saw a single landfill.

Similarly, although we had heard that Corsica was poor, we never came across any visible signs of poverty there. No trailer camps, no shacks, no shantytowns, no street beggars.

What we did see as we biked through the Corsican countryside, and we saw them frequently, were the strange carved rock formations left by prehistoric people -- archeological remains that dot the landscape. Called megaliths or "menhirs," they were discovered in the 1940s. It is conjectured that they were either religious symbols or shelter for the people of the Stone Age who may have put them there (with considerable effort, no doubt) between 6000 BC and 1400 BC. Prehistoric Bronze Age Torreen settlements dating between 1300 BC and 800 BC gradually replaced the megalithic culture.

Almost every day in both Corsica and Sardinia, a cyclist with an interest in prehistory could pull off the road for a quiet rest amid these ancient stone monuments.

At one point in our Corsican bike tour, it was necessary to cross an interior mountain range, an awesome prospect for anyone not on the Tour de France. Happily, our tour company gave us an alternative, and we snaked up the hairpin turns in the back of a van, riding in comfort on a little road that went through the thick, impenetrable "maquis," the same maquis that helped French partisans hide successfully from German troops during World War II.

Up and up we went, through the scrub growth mixed with myrtle, Scotch broom, wisteria, lavender, and the spiky white agapanthus -- which costs $65 per pot if you purchase it at Winston Flowers in Boston, but grows like dandelions in Corsica. Stopping at a restaurant in the mountains for lunch, we could look out across all of Corsica to the Mediterranean, and across the Mediterranean itself to our next destination: Sardinia.

Mid-way through the trip, a motorboat picked us up after breakfast at the dock of our Grand Hotel de Cala Rossa, and we sped along the Corsican coast until we reached the stunning old town of Bonifacio, built on top of 200-foot-high white stone chalk cliffs. (Don't pass up a chance to explore the sea-level grottoes that have been carved out of the cliffs by the waves, if you have the opportunity.)

Then -- following a delicious al fresco lunch at a sidewalk cafe in the old city -- we boarded high-speed cigarette boats for the quick trip to another country, another culture, another language, and another currency.

Geographically, Sardinia is similar to Corsica, though it is slightly larger. It too has the delightfully isolated feeling that only islands bestow upon their inhabitants and visitors. Biking the near-empty roads along the coastline was every bit as blissful as on those of the French island to the north. Waterman-ink-blue ocean to the left, deep green fields to the right, a straight, leisurely road underneath our wheels.

The jewel of Sardinian hotels is the stunning stone and tile Hotel Cala de Volpe on the Costa Smeralda, or Emerald Coast.

When Karim Aga Khan discovered this undeveloped area in the 1960s, he set out to create one of the most exquisite resorts in the world. With the help of architect Jacques Couelle, an extraordinary adobe structure was built in perfect harmony with the land, stretching around the lovely cove where it sits, providing private, sun-filled balconies for every room in a style that is half Moorish, half Mediterranean.

Yachts pull up to the front door, and beautiful people from all over the world play tennis and golf in its back yard. Some of the resort's clientele may have raised their eyebrows when our motley group of bicyclists wheeled up to the gate for one glorious night's stay, but they let us in the front door, regardless, and even into the inner sanctum of the dining room.

Speaking of dining...

Unlike our other European bike trips (Provence and Burgundy come to mind), no one promised gourmet fare on this trip, and we weren't expecting it. In the end, we were pleasantly surprised -- but it was the lunches in Corsica and Sardinia, not the dinners, that made the greatest impression.

How could one forget the midday meal of wild boar, for example, served with slices of dark brown walnut polenta in a rich fruit sauce? That was a specialty in the Swiss Alpine-style restaurant on the top of a mountain in Corsica.

Another lunch featured the classic "soupa Corsa," made of potatoes, cabbage, onions, tomatoes, pasta, and broad beans in a combination that the menu boasts "is so thick you can stand your fork straight up in it." (If you can't, you send it back to the kitchen.)

Then there was the lunch served poolside at the Cala di Volpe where the chef offered live fish swimming in a container. He took your choice back to the kitchen and cooked it to your individual order. That's what's called fresh fish.

And there was the lunch on the terrace of the farmhouse in Corsica that featured an endless succession of antipasti, homemade ravioli, braised mushrooms, julienned and deep-fried sweet zucchini, fresh bread, assorted cheeses and the signature dessert made from bracciu (similar to ricotta cheese). The latter was sprinkled with sugar and *aquavite grappa*. All this, of course, was accompanied by large quantities of red, white and rosé wine in earthenware pitchers. By the time we finished, we could scarcely get back on our bikes.

What about those wines of Corsica and Sardinia?

Well, let's be honest, we're not talking St. Emilion or Margeaux here. But the wines of these islands are certainly pleasant, and some of them have a surprising amount of character. Muscat, a sweet white Corsican wine, makes a particularly nice aperitif, served cold at cocktail time.

So what is there to say about biking in Corsica and Sardinia? Here's what: these two Mediterranean islands are a perfect alternative for the well-traveled vacationer who has been to the Continent before and is looking for something new in a European experience. And biking, incidentally, isn't the only option.

We took an exhilarating seven-mile hike down a deeply forested mountain trail in the heart of Corsica. Another day we journeyed through the countryside of Sardinia on an exquisitely restored steam-driven train, its wood-and-leather

A Corsican village on a rocky coastline.

interior gleaming, its brass fixtures polished to a high gloss.

If you overdose on exercise, by the way, you can always soothe your sore muscles -- as we did -- in the hot sulfur springs of Caldane, where it is believed the Roman centurions used to bathe before going into battle.

Oh yes, about that swimmer...

Her name was Jennifer Figge from Colorado, a friend of several members of our group. She was a former long-distance runner and all-around jock who wanted to become the first American woman to swim from Corsica to Sardinia. She tried to do it the same day we took the journey by the cigarette boat, but bureaucratic red tape got in her way.

Finally, a week later – after spending a total of five hours and 22 minutes in the water – Jennifer made it to Sardinia on her own. By muscle power.

She missed that great lunch on the terrace of the farmhouse, but no one felt sorry for her. She had established a world swimming record – and had memories, as we all did, of those sweet biking days on the roads of Corsica and Sardinia.

ALSACE, FRANCE

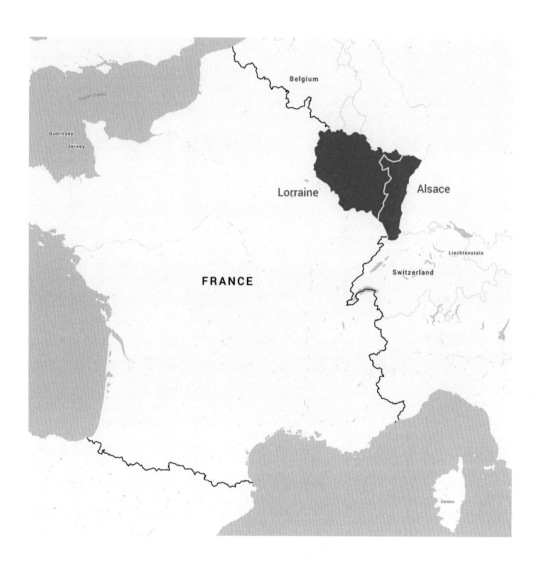

Rest breaks are permitted on bike tours.

Alsace

October, 2000

This time would be different. We'd do it ourselves.

Enjoy it more and pay less. That was the idea, at least. Not that we didn't enjoy our luxury group bicycle tours before. Over the years, we have taken eight of them; three in France, one in Italy, one in Spain, one in Hungary, one in Corsica and Sardinia, and one through the wine region of California.

But we asked ourselves: With all that experience behind us, why couldn't we put together a "luxury" bike trip to France ourselves -- for considerably less money?

That was the challenge. It sounded simple.

Fifteen years ago, in 1984, we took our first Butterfield & Robinson bike tour and wrote about it in The Boston Sunday Globe. At the time, group bike trips of this sort were a novelty, and so was our article, the first to appear on the subject in that newspaper.

Since then, high-end bike trips abroad have become the rage, and for good reason. When you sign up for one, you don't have to think about your bike, your hotel, your luggage, your restaurants, or your route. You simply pay your money (dearly) -- and everything is done for you from that point on. All you have to do is make your feet go around.

Now we asked ourselves: Could we make all these arrangements ourselves, and pedal too?

"You're going to be sorry," a former fellow traveler warned us. "A bike trip to Europe on your own is a huge headache."

What does he know, we thought. No problem.

First question: Where to go? That was easy. We decided to go back to where we began, to France. Specifically to the picturesque little region along the northeast border of France and Germany known as Alsace. And we decided to invite another couple, Jim and Diane Dean, old friends from South Berwick, Maine, who had never biked in Europe before.

The second question in our do-it-yourself bike tour was where to find the bicycles we would ride.

"Take your own bikes," advised a skeptical acquaintance. "We rented ours in Europe and the quality of the bikes was so bad it nearly ruined our trip."

That seemed like good advice. All four of us are "mechanically challenged," shall we say (*how do you put the chain back on when it comes off on a French road in the middle of nowhere?*), so the prospect of dismantling our bikes in Boston and putting them together in Paris did not appeal. Given our incompetence, that could take the length of our trip. We decided to take our chances and rent bikes there.

As it turned out, that was easier said than done. Bike rental shops are not on every street corner in France. It took several long-distance telephone calls in six-grade French before we finally located a rental company near Strasbourg, our jumping-off point in Alsace.

But when the bikes were delivered to our hotel after we arrived, we discovered that they were better than our own at home, shiny black beauties with new panniers hanging on either side of the back wheels, new hybrid tires, 18-speed gears, and a cute little bell off the front handlebar to forewarn pedestrians of our approach. So far, so good.

The next challenge was our luggage. Namely, how to transport it as we toured Alsace on bicycles?

On organized tours, a special van always carries your luggage from one hotel to the next. Why should this be any different? From Boston, the solution seemed obvious: We would rent our own van. Three of our bikes would fit on a standard door rack. The fourth could be crammed inside, along with our baggage. And there would be just enough room left for the four of us.

That was our plan, at least.

Everything started out o.k. When we arrived at Orly Arport we picked up a snazzy green Renault van that looked as though it had plenty of space. It didn't. Three of our bikes went on the rack as planned, but the bike designated for the inside of the van wouldn't fit, nor would our luggage, nor would we. There were too many seats in the way.

We stood in the underground parking lot, our suitcases and the forth bicycle strewn around us. It looked for a few tense moments as if our bike trip was doomed before it began. Everything couldn't fit into this van.

But then, a sudden flash of inspiration. We needed to remove three of the rear seats to make room for the bike, a simple solution. Not quite that simple, as things turned out. After a lot of tugging and pulling and cursing, we finally

Friends Dianne and Jim Dean; Julie at right.

unhinged the seats. That was the easy part. The hard part was persuading the perplexed French rental agent, using our minimal French language skills, to take back three seats and store them in her office until we returned. And that wasn't the only problem we had at the airport. Due to a bank strike, the French exchange bureaus had run out of French francs. But that's another story.

Equipped with our sleek rental bikes and a newly converted van, we finally set off on our first day of do-it-yourself adventure.

A word about Alsace itself. When we told our friends where we were going, their faces usually clouded over with a look of puzzlement. Some had a vague historical memory of Alsace being associated with World War II, but couldn't quite place it. Was that the same Alsace as Alsace-Lorraine?

Yes, but now it's just called Alsace. There's plenty of reason for confusion. The narrow spit of land that runs for 60 miles in the northwest corner of France along the borders of Germany and Switzerland, has been fought over since Roman times, bouncing back and forth depending on who won. It was ravaged during the Thirty Years' War in the 17th century, held by France for two centuries, became a province of Germany in 1870 after the Prussians invaded France, then returned to France at the end of World War I. It was annexed back to Germany in 1940, and finally returned to the French again after the Nazis were defeated in World War II.

It's beautiful enough to merit all the bloodshed. Most Americans are not familiar with Alsatian village names such as Dambach, Illhaeusern, Obernai, and Riquewihr -- and it's their loss, because these are among the most charming European towns.

This is window-box heaven. The villages, with their characteristic half-timbered architecture and brightly colored plaster walls, are overloaded in spring with window boxes filled with geraniums, petunias, marigolds, and other blooms of every size and hue. The towns are awarded "flowers," comparable to the Michelin stars for food, as a rating system for how many beautiful green spaces and flowers they have. Even the bridges over the canals and rivers of the towns are covered with flower boxes.

With the narrow cobblestone streets bathed in sunlight and the ancient walls of the buildings painted green or blue or yellow, the little Alsatian towns look as though Disney had a hand in their creation.

The morning after we arrived, following a restful night in an Alsatian inn with bright red shutters, selecting our day's route was the next order of biking-without-Butterfield business. Organized bike tours typically provide everyone with daily route maps, together with scavenger-hunt-like instructions on how to find that evening's destination. Our self-designed tour didn't provide that benefit. We had to devise our own routes. We would stay in the same place for two nights, taking round-trip tours each day, then drive on to the next inn and repeat the process.

The Bureau of Tourism in Strasbourg gave us a big boost, providing free maps with the "Route des Vins," showing the vineyards marked in red. The routes follow tiny paved roads, marked by signs with bike symbols, winding leisurely through the vineyards and back roads of Alsace. You can follow them for miles, and you're often the only moving thing in sight. When you do see another biker, he or she will most likely not be American. For whatever reason, this area is simply not visited by many tourists from the United States.

Bike trips being what they are, it's easy to get lost, notwithstanding the maps and route signs. And before we even got out of town on that first day, we were. Each of us had a different opinion of how to leave the city and get onto the correct bike route.

After a conference in the middle of a traffic rotary, we finally headed out toward the Vosges Mountains, a distant landmark along the Route des Vins. A big mistake, as it turned out. The road began to slant upward, and then upward more, and more... until it felt as though we must have taken a turn toward the Alps, not the Vosges.

"Whose idea was this road?" one of the husbands asked, panting and sweating profusely as he struggled to reach the top of a particularly steep hill.

"Yours," his wife answered irritably. The others concurred.

Finally, exhausted, we turned around and streaked back down the hill, glorying in the cool air and effortless coasting. Near the bottom, we passed by a "cave," a commercial wine cellar with an open invitation to come in for free samplings of the local vineyard. We accepted the invitation and entered the cool, dark premises for our first tasting of Alsatian white wine, a refreshingly cold, slightly sweet Gewurtztraminer that soon gave us a new lease on life.

The steep climb was forgotten.

The next morning, we decided to play it safe. We bought a colored pen to mark all our maps with the route, and together we wrote out professional tour-style directions for our day's round trip leading back to the same night's lodging:

"1) Take D-35 north to Blienschweller. 2) Go right on D-203. 3) After the overpass, go left on D-703 to Epfig. 4) Go through Epfig on D-603 to St. Marguerite. 5) South on D-603 to D-203. 6) D-203 toward Kogenheim. 7) Cross N-83 and take the first left toward Kogenheim. 8) Out of Kogenheim, take a right onto the unnamed road toward Witterheim."

All this map-marking and direction-making during our breakfast took so long that a member of our little group finally gave up, frustrated. "I'm just going to look for the names of towns, and hope for the best," he declared. That sounded good to the rest of us, too, and for the remainder of the trip that was the system we used. We abandoned written directions and just followed our instincts. We just went where the roads took us, and every day they took us through countless vineyards, past luxurious fields of corn and red poppies, around and through little towns marked on the horizon by tall church steeples, always with the blue silhouette of the Vosges Mountains in the distance.

If one gets lost in Alsace, here's a tip: The ancient castles that sit on the tops of the mountains are excellent reference points, as well as glorious examples of Gothic and Romanesque architecture. You may be going in circles, but these old castles are always in the same place.

And castles aren't the only reason to look up. The beloved storks of Alsace, sitting on their massive nests on the tops of chimneys in the medieval towns, are also a fascinating sight.

Late one morning we wheeled into a flower-filled village with delicate Baroque wrought-iron shop signs, carrying a baguette and a bottle of wine in

Historic architecture is never far away in Europe.

our panniers for lunch. We had settled on a park bench and were passing around hunks of bread with slices of cheese when one of us looked up. Directly overhead was a mother stork surveying us from her nest, providing one of those perfect moments on a bike trip when you think: "I'm living in the moment, and this moment is perfect."

Hey, guess what, you can have these moments with or without benefit of a pricey prepackaged tour.

But not always, it turned out. Not if they involve a spontaneous visit to a beautiful old chateau. On organized tours, we were often ushered into one of those exquisitely preserved 13th-century chateaus that dot the European countryside, welcomed warmly by an owner who would make it available for a picnic luncheon in the inner courtyard. One afternoon on this trip, biking on our own, we came across just such an authentic old chateau and stopped to get a better look. We were instantly greeted by a ferocious Alsatian police dog, accompanied by a scowling caretaker and an owner in a black turtleneck shirt and riding boots to match. All three of them let us know we'd better get the hell off the property. Quickly. Which we did, without looking back. There would be no friendly walkabouts on that property.

There was no problem, however, when it came to finding exceptional restaurants. Alsace is, after all, a gastronomic center, with more Michelin-starred restaurants than any other region in France. The province is a stronghold of "border cooking," blending Franco-Germanic cuisine. You can fall into almost any bistro, as we did, and have a dinner for four people consisting of fish bisque, onion tarts, large green salads, plates of ham knuckle on a huge pile of sauerkraut, baked chicken with a sauce made from Alsatian Riesling wine, homemade noodles, fresh bread, crème caramel, chocolate ice cream, coffee, a bottle of white wine, and large beers -- all for about $20 each.

Nor did we have any difficulties finding quaint and welcoming local inns every night. Some worrywarts at home had warned us it would be impossible to find available hotels along our popular bike route in June without having reservations in advance. But we took our chances and never regretted it. Well, almost never. Until we ran into Whitsunday.

The street outside our hotel on the morning of June 1 seemed strangely quiet when we set off after breakfast. Stopping at a patisserie to pick up a picnic lunch, the girl behind the counter explained that people were sleeping in because it was Whitsunday, or Ascension Day, the beginning of a long holiday weekend not unlike our July 4.

Unconcerned, we purchased white asparagus quiches, apples, apricots, and a bag of fresh sweet cherries, then piled into the van, headed for our next destination. Along the way, we noticed more and more bikers on the road, presumably taking advantage of the holiday weekend.

Where, we wondered, were they all going to stay? The answer came at about five that afternoon, when we decided it was time to find lodging.

They were staying in the little inn we chose for that night... and the next inn... and the next inn.

Every time Tim and Jim went into a B&B to ask for accommodations, leaving Julie and Diane in the van, the word always came back the same:

No room.

Tourists from all over the country, not to mention Germany and Switzerland had apparently booked hotels months in advance for this holiday.

After hearing there was no room for the fifth time, we began to panic. What if we couldn't find lodging in all of Alsace? Would we have to sleep in the crowded van? Or, God forbid, in the grass at the side of the road? Perhaps self-organized bike trips weren't such a hot idea after all.

Julie and Diane conferred, analyzing the situation with female intuition. They wondered if the problem could have anything to do with the way Jim and Tim looked when they approached the innkeeper and asked for a room.

Picture two middle-aged American men, one pudgy, the other skinny, both in skin-tight biking shorts with every bump and lump and bulge of their lower torsos emphasized; add a clashing mosaic of neon colored biking shirts; sprinkle in some bare, hairy legs and clunky biking shoes with white socks; top this image off with foolish, childlike biking caps...

Could this explain why one innkeeper after another gave the same reply? It was always: "Hotel complet." No rooms available.

Julie and Diane came up with a possible solution: Keep Jim and Tim in the van. "We'll go in and make the inquiries ourselves," they said.

In the little town of Chatenois, our next stop, the two wives came back to the van from the local inn with broad smiles on their faces. The ladies had found a room immediately. In fact they had found several rooms. In fact they had found an *inn-full* of rooms.

"The innkeeper was a dear," Julie said. "When we told him our predicament he picked up the phone and called another inn down the street owned by a friend. We couldn't understand what he said, but it was obviously something nice about us. When he hung up he said we could have the whole inn to ourselves for the night."

The innkeeper down the street was just leaving with his family for the holiday weekend but that was no problem. We could stay there anyway. Alone. Sight unseen. He would leave the door unlocked for us. There was only one requirement. We must lock the door and leave the key in a particular crack in an outside brick wall when we left.

By the time we got there, the place was deserted. We opened the front door and found a note on a chair in the lobby, written in wobbly English: "Welcome," it read, "Please feel free to use juice, coffee, bread and jam for breakfast. Make yourselves comfort."

So that's what we did. Made ourselves comfort in an empty inn. We had our choice of eight bedrooms, the run of a clean, well-appointed kitchen and an interior courtyard full of flowers. That evening, on a second-floor balcony that overlooked the garden, we brought out a deck of cards and played a game of bridge.

The silent, dimly-lit inn had an eerie quality. Far into that Whitsunday Eve, the only sounds that broke the stillness were the muffled bids of a universal card game. The ghost of Charles Goren wandered through the inn's empty corridors

"One heart"... "Two clubs"... "Two no- trump"... "Double!"
Biking in Alsace is exceptionally beautiful, and so was the spring weather. On some mornings we felt energetic enough to bike into the hills, and the reward was a quieter, darker road, shaded with forested dales that held pools of cool night air and the pungent fragrance of evergreens. Emerging from the forests, we'd bike through sun-baked vineyards. Smoke from burning brush hung in the hot air, mixed with the sweet smell of ripe grapes.

One day, biking east, we came to the Rhine. We crossed the river, passed a sign on the other side. ACHTUNG. We were in Germany. Such are the porous borders of the European Union these days. By coincidence we found ourselves in the Valley of Munster, which is considered the bicycle capital of Germany. It has twice as many bikes as people, with 100,000 residents biking to work each day. The city center is car-free, and there are even bicycle washing stations.

Alsace is full of picturesque villages.

Munster is also the home of the famous cheese of the same name, and before returning across the border, we stopped at a village shop for a glass of cold Riesling wine and a slice of that same delicious cheese.

That afternoon, on the way to our nighttime lodging, we passed through a still-remaining section of the Maginot Line. The forlorn fortifications, which were futilely erected by the French to keep the Germans out before World War II, were still clearly visible under the growth of vines and weeds.

The Second World War was part of our itinerary the next day as well. In a cold dark rain we drove to Struthof-Natzwiller, the only concentration camp built on French soil. A visit to this horrendous place where 25,000 prisoners died under terrible conditions is extremely moving.

Toward the end of our trip, biking out of Colmar in the morning, we rode for miles in total silence. A thick fog hung over the countryside, encasing barns and steeples in mist. The villages seemed empty, the shutters on the farmhouses closed. At one point, the repetitious song of a distant cuckoo followed us down the road, marking the up-and-down pace of our legs. It is times like these, pedaling along in the stillness of the day, alone with our thoughts, when the rhythm of biking becomes mesmerizing, almost spiritual.

Fifty-five years ago, the very same countryside was anything but still, scene of some of the fiercest fighting of World War II as the advancing Allied armies forced the Germans back to the Rhine. Signs of that combat are still evident along the Alsatian back roads. One occasionally passes more of the cement bunkers that guarded these battlefields, held by the Germans one day, the Allies the next, as the fighting raged back and forth on this strategic piece of real estate.

The bunkers are empty now, silent and deteriorating, sad and incongruous reminders of a brutal conflict in the gentle countryside of Alsace, today a biker's paradise.

NORMANDY, FRANCE

Mont St. Michel is a dramatic biking destination.

Normandy

February, 2007

In December 1944, as the Allies chased Hitler's troops out of France seven months after the D-Day invasion, a frustrated German lieutenant colonel named Jochen Peiper, commander of the 1st SS Panzer Division Regiment, complained that the roads here were "for bicycles, not for tanks."

Riding through Normandy more than 60 years later, we would agree. This countryside along the western coast of France is a bike rider's heaven. There was nothing heavenly about it, of course, for those who invaded it some sixty years ago. Back then, it was pure hell.

We came because we wanted to steep ourselves in World War II history while also enjoying a biking holiday. It's possible to do both when riding through this historic region, stopping to visit the invasion beaches, the battlefields, the moldering bunkers, the memorials to the soldiers who fought here six decades ago to end Nazi tyranny – and the cemeteries. The silent, beautiful cemeteries.

We pedal down pencil-thin lanes bordered by the dense, eight-foot-high hedgerows made famous -- or infamous -- during the first few critical weeks of the Normandy invasion in June 1944. Hedgerows are well named: rows of thick hedges that have grown together for hundreds of years to produce a virtually impregnable boundary line separating farmers' fields in this part of France.

In the old days they were used to keep livestock in. In 1944 they were diabolically efficient in keeping the tanks out. The hedgerows severely restricted the Allied forces' attempts to break out of their beachheads in their drive across Normandy to Paris. The Germans, with time to prepare, used the tangled growth as defensive lines, setting up their machine gun emplacements with deadly fields of fire behind them. It was many weeks before the Americans figured out a way to jury-rig metal rods on the front of their tanks to help bore holes through this armor-like vegetation.

In the peacefulness of these narrow lanes, the underbrush full of birdsongs, it is hard to believe that in WWII this bucolic countryside was the site of so much death and destruction. A few short decades later our days were calm, the weather warm, the fields full of wildflowers. We biked through swaths of brilliant yellow rapeseed, past topiaried wisteria climbing the walls of quaint stone houses, stands of deep purple lilacs, beds of pink coral bells, and stunningly beautiful blue bushes identified by an innkeeper as "ceanothe."

We have seen these wildflowers before. They are an iconic feature of every French bike tour, and we have taken three of them over the past thirteen years. The flowers haven't changed in that period. It's worth noting, however, that the companies offering these biking tours have. For one thing, there are many more of them. When we took our first biking excursion to Bordeaux in 1984 there were only one or two such companies offering this new and exciting way to see a country. Now there are many of them. And they go to many new places. The prices have changed as well. Back when we started, these trips were top of the line, price-wise. They provided nothing but the best -- historic chateau accommodations, five-course gourmet meals, numerous wine tastings. All very elegant -- and all at very elegant prices.

This year we decided to explore a new option. We signed up for an "econo tour," provided by Euro-Bike, a company that specializes in less expensive trips.[2] Econo tours, which are growing in popularity, offer fewer group dinners and smaller hotels, but there is little difference in the overall experience, as far as we can tell. The bikes are the same, the roads are the same, the flowers are the same. Yet the cost is about $1,000 less than the "luxury" tours we first went on. The little hotels are as charming as the Michelin-starred chateaus, and the group meals are every bit as fancy. (They also include the wine, which wasn't always the case on the other trips.) The econo bike tours may be slightly less elegant, but you have a thousand dollars left over for you next bike tour.

The trip started at the Grand Hotel des Thermes in St. Malo on the Brittany coast, with a dinner featuring the tasty fresh mussels and oysters of this area, plus crabmeat in an avocado sauce and an enormous assortment of local cheeses – all of which reminded us why we keep returning to France. The Burgundy wine flowed, as it did at our final dinner. (The latter was held at Le Lion D'Or in Bayeaux, one of the region's best and most expensive restaurants and,

---

[2] *After this article appeared in the Boston Sunday Globe, Euro-Bike was acquired by Austin Adventures.*

In France poppies grow like weeds.

according to historian Stephen E. Ambrose writing in "Citizen Soldiers," General Dwight D. Eisenhower's favorite. Although the staff had no record of what Ike liked, we had no doubt about our favorites: the warm croustade of Camembert, the poached white fish in a Granny Smith apple sauce, and the mille-feuille of pear and crepe with caramel ice cream and pear sorbet.)

After breakfast in Brittany on the second day of the trip,, we had followed signs to Normandy and shortly after crossing the border saw in the distance one of the most recognizable landmarks in all of France -- Mont Saint-Michel, the tidal island Romanesque monastery built in the eighth century. This stunning cathedral, surrounded by a medieval village, used to be cut off from the mainland by high tides, which turned the ocean waters into its own private moat. Nowadays there is a causeway allowing visitors to walk or take a shuttle to this historic place, which in 1979 was added to the UNESCO list of World Heritage Sites.

Before leaving on our trip, we had read several histories of the D-Day invasion to prepare for what we would see. That kind of research is always a good idea, but there is something about Normandy that speaks to the visitor without need for reference books. History is ever-present here.

We knew we had arrived near the invasion site when we began to notice small white plaques on the side of the road. Each one told the story of a young life that had ended on that terrible day. The roads bore their names. "Olle Road," was one of the first we came to. It was named, according to the plaque, "in honor of T/5 S.J. Olle, 531st Engineer Shore Regiment who was killed in action June 6, 1944."

More and more of these little markers came into view as we biked along, and we also began to pass bunkers -- massive cement hulks, still intact, buried in the earth. We took refuge in one during a sudden rain squall, climbing down the steps to huddle in the damp, dark space below. Who had huddled inside that same dark, damp space in June of 1944, we wondered. What were their names, the young Germans who had peered out of the firing slits at the advancing Americans? What were they feeling?

Then, suddenly, we reached Omaha Beach. Today it is a wide, sandy expanse where the waves splash gently on the sand. But at 6:30 a.m. on June 6, 1944, it was hell on earth. Thousands died here before the day was over. The Omaha Beach Museum on a hill overlooking the sea memorializes the bloody Normandy invasion through films, photographs, scale models, documents, and equipment displays.

On another day we biked to Arromanches, where the Allies constructed an artificial harbor for ships to unload men and materiel in support of the invasion. The Cinema Circulaire dramatically brings the sights and sounds of war to life with a 360-degree screen that puts one in the middle of the action. For anyone interested in World War II history, it shouldn't be missed.

Nearby, we stood in the bunker made famous in the scene from the film "The Longest Day" when German soldiers caught their first glimpse of the immense Allied invasion armada heading toward them in the early morning gloom. All around us were deep craters from the bombs dropped by our planes in that spring of 1944.

Each day's bike route brought us to a cemetery, a beach, a bunker, or a museum that memorialized this savage time. One of the most dramatic sights of all -- save for the thousands of poignant marble crosses at the American Cemetery -- was the life-size model of a soldier hanging by his parachute harness

A peaceful village now but not during World War II.

from the church steeple in the little town of Ste. Mere Eglise. That was American paratrooper John Steele, who dangled there for three hours on the night of June 6 until his fellow paratroopers rescued him. An excellent museum sits across the street from the now world-famous church.

Euro-Bike provided us each morning with maps of the route we were to take, as well as plenty of historical background material on the area. In addition, our delightful Dutch guide, Loek Toepoel, offered us a cellphone to put into our bike bag in case we got lost, something that happens often on these winding little roads. We didn't need it, however. We had brought our own phone, a high-tech model that allowed us to ring up our children in the States and talk to them thousands of miles away while standing beside our bikes in the middle of Normandy. Such has been the amazing advancement of international communications. On our first trip, 23 years ago, we scribbled three-line messages to our loved ones in the States on the backs of postcards, which arrived two weeks later... if at all.

It is not uncommon, these many years after the war, for older French people in Normandy to wave at passing American bikers and shout a grateful "merci" for the sacrifices our soldiers made to liberate their country a generation ago. Of course there are exceptions to every rule, and we were saddened to confront one of them near the end of our trip one afternoon when Toepoel backed our tour van a few feet into a residential driveway to turn around.

The lady owner appeared out of nowhere, screaming "private property!" and proceeded to bang furiously on the side of the vehicle. She wrenched the door open to get at poor Toerpel, who was trying to edge the van back onto the road. Now her husband came running up to the van, fists clenched, and tried to pull Toerpel out of his seat. One of our fellow bikers jumped out of the passenger side and came to his defense.

How ironic were the screams of "private property!" we thought as we sped away. With better language skills we would have pointed out that we Americans were the people who made it possible for them to *have* their "private property."

Oh well. Merde happens. Most of the French we encountered on their liberated soil were very gracious, welcoming the Americans who now come to their countryside on bicycles, rather than tanks.

THE NETHERLANDS

Flowers abound in Holland.

Holland

October, 2010

You see them from the air as you fly into Amsterdam. Multicolored bar codes, brilliantly striped.

You see them in bicycle baskets, carried home on some of the 600,000 bikes in Amsterdam, and draped like necklaces over the front grills of buses and baby carriages.

You see them piled on the tops of family cars, a celebratory ornament, not at all funereal.

And, if you happen to be in Haarlem on the night of the spring festival parade, you will see hundreds of thousands of them in every possible color, meticulously attached to huge motorized floats moving through the streets behind blaring bands.

Tulips.

They're synonymous with the Netherlands, so important that when a new variety is developed, one that shows a distinct trait, the growers hold a ceremony to make the name official.

There is a tulip named for a beer -- the "Coors" tulip, exalting the US brewing family whose corporate colors happen to be red and white. "Having a tulip named for our family is quite an honor," said Holly Coors, who sprinkled the namesake blossom with champagne in the traditional "christening" ceremony.

There is also the "Audrey Hepburn Tulip," the "Hillary Clinton Tulip," the "Rembrandt Tulip," and thousands of others of this botanical gem that arrived here from Turkey in the 16th century.

Tulips in bloom are what drew us here this year, our ninth European bike trip since 1985.

Legend has it that the first Dutchman who saw a tulip bulb mistook it for an onion and ate it, tossing others into his tiny vegetable garden. Under Nazi occupation at the end of World War II, the Dutch ate quantities of bulbs in order to survive the "hunger winter" they went through. Today, 40,000 acres - the equivalent of nearly 1,700 Boston Public Gardens -- are devoted to growing tulips in this country.

For anyone biking here in spring they are a stunning sight: rows and rows of brilliant reds, pinks, purples, and yellows crisscrossing the countryside in military precision. And there is another remarkable feature of the Netherlands at tulip time. It strikes you, almost physically, as you pedal through the countryside:

Fragrance.

In late April the beds of tulips look like giant bar codes.

The Dutch grow fields and fields of hyacinths in addition to tulips, and you smell them well before you see them, an overpowering perfume that has a palpable presence. They're some of the most sweetly scented flowers in the world.

The combination of sight and scent makes Holland one of Europe's most delightful destinations for all visitors. But for travelers on two wheels there is an added attraction – something else that is especially appealing about the country: its bike paths. They're among the flattest in the world.

If you think you are too old, too weak, or too stiff to bicycle in Europe, you haven't experienced biking in the Netherlands. It's as flat -- we can't help ourselves -- as a Dutch pancake. You almost feel like you're biking downhill, especially if you're pedaling a $2,000 Cannondale with 27 gears provided by Austin-Lehman Adventures, our tour company on this trip.

Because nearly everyone in the Netherlands owns a bike, the country is laced with thousands of miles of bike trails, and they're almost all paved, smooth, and scenic. We have biked in France, Italy, Spain, Austria, Hungary, Corsica, Sardinia, and Napa Valley, and they all offer superb biking trails. But when it comes to variety and maintenance, the ones in this country are in a league of their own.

They took us past gentle coastal sand dunes with sailboats in the distance, and through dark hardwood forests smelling, oddly, of wintergreen. We rode them along the tops of the ever-present dikes, and beside canals, where women rowed together in two-seat sculls painted bright red and blue; and every day, around noon, they led us into little villages, where we stopped for a lunch of assorted Dutch cheeses on baked bread, still warm from an unseen oven in back of the family shops. Some of the gourmands in our group also ordered smoked eel sandwiches, a Dutch specialty requiring a more adventurous stomach. (Ours are wimpy.) Midafternoon brings a coffee break with another Dutch treat: warm, puffy "poffertiejs" -- silver-dollar-sized pancakes buried in powdered sugar.

The last week in April is prime time to see flowers in bloom here. That's also the best time to see the large variety of migrating birds that are attracted to the country's wetlands. The canals are full of green-headed mallards, hooded mergansers, black scaup with the characteristic white headbands, and pink-billed greylag geese. Black-headed laughing gulls and squabbling terns feed in the waters of the bays.

The lush green fields are also full of nesting swans, stretching their long white necks to pull out clumps of juicy grass, munching on them like grazing cows. Magpies flash back and forth across the trails, their black and white plumage resembling flying whoopie pies.

Even cars in the Netherlands are covered with flowers in Spring.

But for us, the best bird-watching of all took place in the stork refuge located on the premises of the luxurious Chateau de Havixhorst, where we stayed on the fifth night of our trip. A pair of the comical, ungainly birds had built their nest of twigs on top of the chateau's chimney, and the characteristic click-clack of their red bills, sounding like Spanish castanets, woke us in the morning.

In all, we biked 172 miles through four provinces, taking in as many sights and sounds and scents as possible from the vantage of our slowly turning wheels.

The beauty of biking through a foreign country instead of speeding through it in a car is that you have the time to appreciate what you pass.

We visited the storybook village of Giethoorn, known as the "Venice of Holland," where the vehicles are boats and the streets are canals. Hansel-and-Gretel thatch roofed houses looked out on humpback bridges that are a challenge to cross on bikes.

We bicycled past "hunebedden" -- megalithic tombs that are older than England's Stonehenge and Egypt's pyramids. Their rocks were pushed down from Scandinavia by glaciers 200,000 years ago.

Of course we visited one of Holland's iconic windmills, a gigantic working machine at the edge of a marsh. We crept up the narrow stairs to the top floor, where the gears creaked and squealed as the blades outside turned in the wind.

We spent an afternoon at the Frans Hals Museum, repository of the largest collection of paintings by that famous Dutch master. His 17th century portraits still dazzle the eye. There is a full complement of his work at the museum, although perhaps his most acclaimed, the "Gypsy Girl," resides in the Louvre in Paris.

Hals art was uplifting. What we saw one drizzly afternoon, biking through a dark forest, was not. One of our tour guides led us to an underground hiding place in the woods used by Jews when the Nazis occupied the Netherlands

It's hard to resist picking flowers in Keukenhof Gardens.

during the Second World War. Standing there in our garish nylon riding gear, looking down at the cave-like pit once crammed with desperate people, seemed incongruous. The pain and terror of those who lived for months in that miserable place could still be felt.

But Holland is not a place of grief. In the end, it will be the flowers of the Netherlands that remain in our memories. Our trip ended the way it began, surrounded by tulips. We were in Keukenhof Gardens on the outskirts of Haarlem, considered by many the most beautiful spring gardens in the world. Picture 4.5 million tulips in 100 varieties, along with many other radiant flowers densely planted in asymmetrical beds amid tall trees and stunning sculptures.

Babies in strollers, disabled veterans in wheelchairs, American bikers on holiday all shared the sights and scents of this lovely place. Our guide had trouble getting our group to leave. We all hated climbing back on our bikes for the ride to the hotel and our farewell dinner. It wasn't until late in the afternoon that everyone – except the two of us – had pedaled away.

We hung back, wanting to stay in this magical place until the last possible second. But finally, we had to go. On the way to our bikes, we wandered into a little gift shop next to the gate. There, on a table beside the door, we noticed a stack of small paper bags containing tulip bulbs for sale. We don't know anything about tulips. We've never planted them, but we bought three bags. We'll dig them into the ground when we get back to Boston and hope for the best. With a little luck they'll burst into bloom next spring and transport us back to this special country with its lovely bike paths and explosion of April color.

AUSTRIA & THE CZECH REPUBLIC

Parked bikes, at rest in a Czech square.

Vienna to Prague

December, 2013

Do senior citizens have to turn in their bikes and call it quits when they pass the 70-year milestone?

In their eighth decade of life, can they keep up with hotshot young bikers on a European bike tour?

We say no to the first question, yes to the second -- and we're living proof of them both.

For the last 30 years we've been up and down the roads of Europe and California on bicycles, relying on our pedal power. During this interval we passed the middle-age mark. Now we're skirting the old-age mark. Hey, let's face it, we're dangerously close to the assisted-living mark.

As New Year's Day arrived in 2013 we were resigned to the likelihood that our biking days in Europe were over. It wasn't a new thought. We'd had the same one three years earlier, in 2011, when it first dawned on us that perhaps we had reached the end of the road, biking-wise. It was a most depressing conclusion, one we hated to accept. There were a lot of places we still wanted to bike. Tuscany, for example. Beautiful, everyone said, but filled with killer hills. We weren't in the market for killer hills any longer, if we ever were.

In the end we came up with a brilliant solution, a perfect destination for one more bike trip: the Netherlands, a country as flat as a you-know-what. We could handle that. Even at our advanced age, we assured ourselves, a bike trip there should pose no difficulty... and we were right! Biking in Holland felt as if we were coasting downhill all the way. We made it to the end, no problem.

That brings us back to 2013, three years later (and three years older).

Now one of us was approaching his 76th birthday, and we really were ready to hang up the biking shoes. It had been great fun while it lasted, but... our pedal power had run out.

Hadn't it?

At a dinner party one cold night in February we heard a younger couple talking about a European bike trip they had taken the past spring. It went from Vienna to Prague, paralleling the Danube River part of the way. We had never been to Prague, but it was near the top of our bucket list. We had never seen the Danube, either. Ditto.

It sounded absolutely sublime, but...

"There's one problem," the wife noted. "That route is filled with hills. We'd never make it."

She was right.

Well, no, she was wrong, as it turned out. A few weeks later we discovered a new set of "muscles," and shortly thereafter signed up for that very trip, a tour offered by Austin Adventures scheduled for July. In the end we made it all the way to Prague. Easily.

Our rejuvenated muscles were part of a newfangled bike we learned about and rode on that trip for the first time, hopefully not the last. Austin Adventures had given us the secret to success when we called to inquire about the route.

"We're not sure we can make it," we said. "We're old."

"Not to worry," the representative had replied. "We have just the bikes for you. They're electric bikes. You'll love them."

And he was right. We did.

Senior citizens take note:

If you still crave adventure mixed with exercise, if you biked the hilly roads of Tuscany in your younger days and rode up to the beautiful hilltop chateaus of Provence, don't give up now. They're still within reach of your biking biceps.

You've mastered e-mail, banked by e-commerce, read e-books and bought an e-car. Now it's time to enter the wonderful world of e-bikes.

A 205-mile bike hike up and down the hills stretching from Vienna, Austria, to the city of Prague in the Czech Republic? Piece of cake. Piece of Sacher cake.

We biked there without breaking a sweat. Well, ok, maybe a little one. With our little e-secret, we found ourselves at the head of our group's straggling peloton going up the steepest inclines.

Electric bikes look like any other except for a small lithium battery -- the size and shape of a loaf of ciabatta bread -- on a carrying rack over the rear tire. Unlike a motorbike, they make no noise. Unless you reveal your secret, other bikers have no idea your bicycle is on hidden steroids.

Riders on these magical machines still have to pedal, of course, like everyone else, and the bikes have the usual gears that one shifts going uphill and downhill. But the electric-assisted bikes have another lever that allows you to choose one of four levels of help with the flick of your thumb on the handlebar: ECO gives you a gentle lift as you bike along a flat vineyard road. TOUR adds a little more

Every dessert in the Czech Republic is a work of art.

zip at the start of a long hill. SPORT ups the ante another notch as you begin to pant on a steep incline... and TURBO puts you over the top in racing mode, where you bomb up hills like a Tour de France champion, speeding past all the other poor devils gasping for air as they toil upward.

Our original plan was to move back and forth between our e-bike and our regular gears depending on that day's terrain. Once we had used the e-gears, however, it was harder and harder not to click that first "Eco" lever at the start of each day's ride. Even the macho-male husband eventually gave into the temptation.

Using an e-bike reminds you of your childhood. It feels like your dad is helping you learn to ride a two-wheeler, running behind you, pushing you along with an invisible hand. When you falter, he gives you a gentle shove from the rear.

"Pedal!" he whispers in your ear. "Keep pedaling! Don't worry about the hill. I'll help you!"

Sometimes that help caused unanticipated problems. Early in the trip, one of us was using the electric gears (ok, let's be specific, it was the wife) and the other was still using the conventional system, laboring up a killer incline. Call it male pride. *No need to rely on electronic help,* he thought, *I can do this myself. I'm no wimp.* Upping the level of her battery assistance, the wife shot up the hill so fast that she left her sweating, struggling partner far behind, not realizing she had zipped past the turnoff in the route directions. Ten minutes and a few turns later, up and over the top of the hill, she realized that her husband was not with her. What's more, neither was her route map. She was lost.

Meanwhile, the husband had come to a panting stop on the hill's incline and was waiting for his wife to reappear. He waited. And he waited. And he waited some more, muttering a few maledictions about his female traveling partner. Finally he saw her coasting downhill, somewhat sheepishly, trying to find him.

It's always fun to get a little lost on one of these bike tours -- but not when you're stranded on the side of a steep hill, not sure whether to go up or down, wondering where your wife is. The husband was slightly peeved but he quickly calmed down and turned on his own lithium battery for the rest of the day.

Many of our earlier European bike trips (the first one was in 1984) had been taken in springtime, the fragrance of mown grass and the rich wet earth of furrowed fields heavy in the air as the planting season began. This trip was in the fall, at the height of the harvest, and the sights and smells were different. We biked past apple and pear trees heavy with fruit; past vineyards in the Wachau wine region, their vines thick with blue and green grapes; past orchards hanging with sweet purple plums and ripe yellow peaches.

"Pedal!" Dad whispered in our ear. "Keep pedaling! Don't worry, I'll help you!"

And so we continued pedaling. We pedaled through rich Austrian farmland. We pedaled on a winding track beside the Danube River in a throng of runners competing in a marathon. We pedaled in the dark pine-scented Bohemian Forest, not a soul around. We rode past a gypsy colony near the medieval town of Cesky Kremlov. We biked up to the Hluboka Castle, one of the many majestic early Gothic structures in the Czech Republic, and we tackled an even steeper incline to reach Stift Gottweig, the stunning Baroque Benedictine monastery in Lower Austria.

In this part of the world, all the many castles, abbeys and monasteries that dot the landscape sit atop the hilliest part of the countryside. Allegedly, the residents wanted to be closer to heaven. Whenever we headed up one we had to control a childish temptation to stick our tongue out at the other (much younger) bikers who were huffing and puffing their way up to the summit as we

Vineyards and historic buildings compete for attention.

merrily passed by.

On and on we went, our e-bikes making life on the road smooth and easy. Even with e-bikes, of course, 70-year-olds occasionally need a little energy boost, and whenever that happened one of the Austin Adventures guides would suddenly appear at the top of a hill with a plate of Austrian chocolates or a dish of fresh Czech apricots or a cold fruit drink to give us a quick shot of energy.

Remember those hotshot young bikers who were going to leave us in their dust? They didn't.

The ones we'd never be able to keep up with? We did.

In our eighth decade of life we never gave up or out. Thanks to invisible help from our friend we biked 200-plus miles in all. It felt like a short trip to the store at home.

Many Europeans have already embraced e-bikes for commuting to work. ("They allow me to bike to my office without perspiring and needing a shower when I arrive," explained a young Czech man we met on the road.) Granted, the lithium battery makes them heavier. Our creaky backs might have a hard time lifting one of these bikes onto a car rack at home.

But ahhh, what benefits these magic machines bestow on a European bike tour. For seniors like ourselves, e-bikes represent an exciting new opportunity: They could extend our biking lifetime another 10 years.

On to Tuscany!

Bikers become old friends by the end of every tour.

Acknowledgments

No writer can ever claim full credit for the book he or she has written -- or he *and* she, in our case. The birth of a book is almost always a team effort, and this one was no exception. Given its thirty-years gestation, we can't acknowledge all those who helped bring *Thirty Years on Two Wheels* to life. But the following are high on our list:

The Boston Globe, our employer for a collective total of 55 years, published our first article in 1984 and each one thereafter, displayed prominently in the Sunday Travel Section. For that -- and much more during our careers at the Globe -- we are grateful. Special thanks to former Globe Travel editor Bill Davis and his successor, Jerry Morris for their care in editing those early pieces, and the later ones as well.

We also owe thanks to the companies that pioneered bicycle tours in the first place, a new idea when we began these journeys.

Butterfield & Robinson, the biking company whose European tours first made us fall in love with the concept of slow travel down beautiful vineyard lanes, encouraged us to pursue the idea of a book based on the original articles in the Globe, and opened up its photo archives to provide us with a number of images to fill in the blanks of our own collection. Special thanks in that connection to Katie Marshall, who always came up with just what we were looking for.

Liz Einbinder and Matt Orendorff of Backroads, another excellent tour company, also dug into their files for photos, especially of the California scenes we biked without a camera in our hands at the time.

We chose a more economical tour when we set off for Normandy, and Euro Bike was the company that led us through that part of France. Soon afterward, Euro Bike was purchased by Austin-Lehman, which later organized our tour through the Netherlands. We are grateful to Carol Austin, one of its founders, for the help she has given us over the years on that trip and others, including our tour of the Czech Republic. By then, her company was named Austin Adventures but it featured the same knowledgeable guides and well-planned itineraries (not to mention those wonderful secret batteries that made us fly up the hills under e-power).

Thirty Years on Two Wheels would never have come to pass without the experiences these tour companies provided, and the opportunity to write about them offered by the Globe. But for the actual creation of the book itself, our hero is Sasha Leland, whose computer skills were a godsend to his technically-challenged parents, and whose wise counsel on everything from formatting to content we depended on every step of the way.

Tim Leland and Julie Hatfield
Boston, Massachusetts
October 14, 2016

Photo Credits

About the Authors

TIMOTHY LELAND is a retired former managing editor and assistant to the publisher of The Boston Globe. During a distinguished 35-year career at the Globe, he covered the first NASA space shots at Cape Canaveral as the newspaper's science reporter, served as its State House bureau chief covering state and local politics, and founded the Globe's long-running full-time investigative team known as "Spotlight," which won a Pulitzer Prize under his leadership in its first year of existence and is featured in a Hollywood film of the same name. He considers his greatest achievement at the paper, however, to be his successful courtship of Julie Hatfield, the Globe's society editor, whom he married in 1984. They took their first of many European bike trips together the following year.

JULIE HATFIELD was a fashion editor, lifestyle writer and society writer for The Boston Globe before "retiring" to become a freelance travel writer for a variety of publications, including the Globe. She is the mother of three and grandmother of five. In her 30 years of biking in different parts of the world, she has had just one accident, when she turned the corner too fast cycling out of her home driveway and broke her left wrist. She was approximately twenty feet from her front door.

14641058R00083

Made in the USA
Lexington, KY
09 November 2018